Tremblay

Negotiating Identities
Women in the Indian Diaspora

Negotiating Identities
Women in the Indian Diaspora

Aparna Rayaprol

DELHI
OXFORD UNIVERSITY PRESS
CALCUTTA CHENNAI MUMBAI
1997

Oxford University Press, Walton Street, Oxford OX2 6DP

Oxford New York
Athens Auckland Bangkok Calcutta
Cape Town Chennai Dar es Salaam Delhi
Florence Hong Kong Istanbul Karachi
Kuala Lumpur Madrid Melbourne Mexico City
Mumbai Nairobi Paris Singapore
Taipei Tokyo Toronto

and associates in

Berlin Ibadan

ISBN 0 19 564151 5

Typeset by Resodyn, New Delhi 110070
Printed in India at Pashupati Printers, Delhi 110032
and published by Manzar Khan, Oxford University Press
YMCA Library Building, Jai Singh Road, New Delhi 110001

For Peelu

Preface

I arrived in Pittsburgh from India in August 1988 as a new bride as well as a new doctoral student in sociology at the University of Pittsburgh. Almost a week after I came to Pittsburgh, it was time to celebrate a Hindu festival Varalakshmi *puja*, which is considered especially important for South Indian married women, and my mother had socialized me to do it. An Indian woman came and took me and my husband to the local Sri Venkateswara temple for a communal celebration of this *puja*.

My initial reaction was one of curiosity as I was wondering how this domestic Hindu ritual could be celebrated in a temple. I discovered how religion and religious rituals take on new meanings for immigrants and how, as they attempt to reproduce the culture back home, that culture gets transformed. Many Hindu immigrants I have met in my five years in Pittsburgh feel it is fortunate to be living in a place where one of the largest temples outside India is located. I was fascinated with what I saw at the temple that night — the women deeply immersed in the *puja*, dressed in their finest silks and gold jewelery, the men running around busily carrying baskets of flowers needed for the *puja*, and the children chatting excitedly with each other. The scene and the joyful expressions of all the participants reminded me of a wedding atmosphere back home in India.

Following this initial visit, we started going to the temple more often, especially for good music and dance concerts. We had to get used to the frequency of these visits as we rarely went to temples in India. In Pittsburgh, however, even people like my not-so-religious husband found themselves wishing to go to the temple once in a while. One thing I observed on every visit was the conspicuous presence of women. Women seemed to be in charge, controlling and managing almost everything.

In the spring of 1990 when I had to do a project for a graduate course in qualitative methods, I decided to engage in participant observation at the S.V. temple and interview the women who visited it frequently. I got so involved and excited with my initial findings that I decided to continue my research and convert it into a dissertation project. I wanted to understand the presence and participation of women in a traditionally patriarchal setting such as a Hindu temple and therefore decided to do an ethnographic study at the S.V. temple.

This study about the South Indian community in Pittsburgh would have been impossible without the co-operation of the immigrants. I am deeply indebted to all of them. They took me into their confidence, let me into their homes, invited me to functions, and bore with all my inquiries. I am especially thankful to my respondents, whose names I cannot mention here for the sake of confidentiality. They not only answered my questions with utmost patience, but also introduced me to other respondents and opened my eyes to several aspects of their lives that eventually found their way into my work. I am grateful to many people in the community for their hospitality. They fed me delicious meals and nurtured me when I most needed it. Several members of the Sri Venkateswara temple's administration provided a friendly atmosphere that facilitated this study. They spent their time and energy to explain the temple's administrative structure and other intricacies of its management. I am grateful to them.

This book would never be what it is today without Dr Lynn Davidman's constant and invaluable guidance. Her immense patience and her characteristic purple ink all over my drafts will remain etched in my memory. She pushed me when I tended to slacken and enthusiastically encouraged me. Her commitment to feminist research and ethnography inspired me to select the topic and led me to the wonderful new world of feminist theory and research.

I would like to thank Dr Roland Robertson, Dr Burkart Holzner, Dr Fred Clothey and Dr Barbara Miller for reading my work and commenting on it at different stages of the document. Professor Ratna Naidu at the University of Hyderabad has been my teacher and provided me the intellectual foundations in sociology. She has read parts of the book and offered valuable advice on organization of chapters.

I would like to thank among my colleagues in Pittsburgh, Philip Mabry for his quiet encouragement and for bringing several interesting readings to my notice. Phil also read and commented upon some of my writings. Thanks also to Denise da Silva, Grace Wang, and Kalpana Biswas for reading and commenting on different chapters of this work. Juliana Martinez and Geetha Srikantan have been willing sounding boards for many of my problems and have been constant sources of support. Special thanks to my family in the United States, the Mallis — Ken, Sophie, David, and Megan. Ken was always there to provide words of encouragement and the family provided a lot of fun and care during my five years at Pittsburgh. I am more than grateful to Mr N.M. Reddy and Mrs Rathnamala Reddy for putting me up in their home and taking care of me during the four months that I was alone in Pittsburgh.

My father urged me to study at an American institution like he did over four decades ago, and my mother taught me to become an independent woman. My sisters have both been encouraging and supportive in their own special ways as was my aunt, Lalitha. I am indebted to my fellow sociologist and husband Vinod Pavarala. He not only read and carefully edited and formatted several drafts of this document at various stages, but also helped me organize my thoughts. I couldn't have done any of this without Vinod's efforts and support.

My thanks to the anonymous reviewer for OUP for his/her valuable suggestions on an earlier draft. Finally, I express my gratitude to Ms Esha Béteille for her persistence and encouragement.

Aparna Rayaprol

University of Hyderabad

Contents

Tables

I

The Indian Diaspora: Metaphor and Reality

Diaspora: (Greek, Dispersion) Members of any religious body, living as a minority, whether in or outside their home-land, and maintaining contact with central authorities of that body.

— Encyclopedic Dictionary of Religion, 1966–70

Diaspora: Jewish communities living in exile outside of Palestine. The Hebrew word for diaspora (galut) means 'exile' (i.e. from the Holy Land) and, though it refers to the physical dispersal of the Jews throughout the world, it also carries religious, philosophical, political and eschatalogical connotations, inasmuch as a special relationship is understood between the land of Israel and the Jewish people.

— Encyclopaedia Britannica [Micropedia]

In a world of diaspora, transnational cultural flows, and mass movements of populations, old-fashioned attempts to map the globe as a set of culture regions or homelands are bewildered by a dazzling array of postcolonial simulacra . . . as India and Pakistan reappear in postcolonial simulation in London . . . and a thousand similar cultural dreams are played out in urban and rural settings all across the globe.

— Gupta and Ferguson, 1992:10

Nations and cultures, long-defined by geography and territory, are undergoing rapid transformation in the late twentieth century. The pace of border-crossings has risen to a new crescendo, with migrants seeking to transfigure cultural boundaries and recreate new representations of their selves, their pasts, and their new milieu. Often, for the increasing numbers of middle-class professionals arriving in the West, immigration is a self-imposed exile driven by economic and social aspirations. However, in the contemporary world of transnational cultural exchanges, movements of people between nations is no longer an exile in any complete sense. Identities and cultures get delocalized, but rarely detached from memories of past places and times. The newly reconstructed identities arising out of transnational migrations — the Jamaican in Queens, the Vietnamese in San Francisco, the Punjabi in Toronto, the Cuban in Miami, and so on — are based on memories that are diverse, selective, and particular.

In the face of such reconfigurations of the global cultural map, scholars are compelled to question the value of the root and 'arboreal' metaphors used to explain 'culture' and replace them with images of 'disjuncture' and 'rupture' (Malkki 1992; Gupta and Ferguson 1992).[1] The 'spatially incarcerated native' (Appadurai 1988) is suddenly freed as anthropologists and sociologists have begun to discover that the 'native's' culture is now spread far and wide and that the 'Third World' now occupies a space within the 'First'. The disjuncture between place and culture cannot be characterized either as a mere homogenization of cultures (e.g. 'Americanization' or 'Westernization' of the world or the 'melting pot' thesis) or as a heterogeneous blooming of distinctive identities independent of one another (e.g. the metaphor of 'salad bowl' in the US). In Geertz's (1986) memorable phrase, 'like nostalgia, diversity is not what it used to be'. People evoke the past in highly selective ways and construct a present that is a hybrid of multiple cultures and experiences. As a result, neither nostalgia nor diversity remain unproblematically pure and simple.

The 'homelands' people reconstruct tend to be fictive communities, part real and part imagined. In *Imaginary Homelands*, Rushdie writes of the sense of loss felt by exiles and expatriates and their urge to reclaim what was lost. In this process of reclamation, he says,

---

[1] Malkki discusses in detail how 'arboreal' or 'arborescent' (tree-like) metaphors have been used to explain people's connections with places. People derive their identities from their ties to a nation, conceptualized as 'a grand genealogical tree, rooted in the soil that nourishes it'. According to Malkki, the metaphor of a tree 'evokes both temporal continuity of essence and territorial rootedness'.

we will not be capable of reclaiming precisely the thing that was lost; . . . we will, in short, create fictions, not actual cities or villages, but invisible ones, *imaginary homelands, Indias of the mind*. . . . (Rushdie 1991).

Identities and memories get transformed over time and, as a result, they tend to be subjective constructions of reality rather than objectively fixed phenomena (Gillis 1994). Robertson (1992:104) explains this global condition as one in which we are participants in a process involving 'the universalization of particularism and the particularization of universalism'. This tension between the universal and the particular can be seen on the one hand, in the scores of Hindu temples dotting the American suburban landscape and on the other, in the use of electronic bulletin boards by Palestinians in exile or expatriate Irish to promote particularisms such as nationalist or fundamentalist movements back home.[2]

The deterritorialized identities of refugees, immigrants, and other displaced peoples, facing what Said (1979) has called 'a generalized condition of homelessness', are reconstructed in imaginative ways in their new environments. For thousands of these displaced persons, it is a journey from the ex-colony to the post-colony where they experience and express their nostalgia for the past in various forms. As Gupta and Ferguson (1992) point out, Anderson's (1983) idea of 'imagined communities' assumes a new meaning and life in the immigrant context.

[I]t becomes most visible how imagined communities come to be attached to imagined places, as displaced peoples cluster around remembered or imagined homelands, places, or communities in a world that seems increasingly to deny such firm territorialized anchors in their actuality. . . . Remembered places have often served as symbolic anchors of community for dispersed people. This has long been true of immigrants, who use memory of place to construct imaginatively their new lived world (Gupta and Ferguson 1992:10–11).

A central problematic in any work on immigrant cultures is: how does one conceptualize the process of reconstruction? As Liisa Malkki (1992) points out, the dominant metaphor to describe the relocation of peoples and cultures has been botanical, that of 'transplantation'. For example, titles of books on Indian immigrants, such as *The Banyan Tree* (Tinker 1977) and *Transplanting*

---

[2] The idea of 'electronic nationalism' is borrowed from a lecture by Benedict Anderson delivered at the University of Pittsburgh in 1992.

Religious Traditions (Fenton 1988) suggest that the relocation of immigrants is a smooth journey of people who neatly pack their roots and 'transplant' them later in an orderly manner in the new society. Such a representation glosses over the fact that immigration constitutes an epistemological crisis of great magnitude, involving changes in legal and political status, ruptures in families, struggles for economic mobility, and tensions between the older social and cultural values and the norms and values of the new society. As I suggested earlier, the process of reconstruction of communities is better conceptualized as a rupture or a disjunctive crisis. These crises take different forms and my focus in this book will be on gender relations and religious identities in a particular section of the diaspora. Before I examine the ways in which the immigrants deal with this crisis, it is necessary to briefly trace the history of the Indian diaspora.

THE INDIAN DIASPORA

The term 'Indian diaspora' is generally used to refer to migrants who originated in areas falling within the territorial boundaries of present-day India (Parekh 1993). For this purpose, it is said to be irrelevant whether these migrants identify themselves as 'Indian', politically or otherwise. Nadarajah (1994) problematizes the naming of the transnational community of Indians, which he says is not merely cultural but also political. For instance, the pejorative 'coolie' is embedded in the orientalist discourse. The 'diasporizing' of Indians dispersed in different parts of the world by Bhikhu Parekh and others probably stems from certain political, economic, and cultural conditions. Indians abroad, unlike immigrants of other nationalities, have maintained negligible horizontal linkages with one another. The usage of the umbrella label, 'diaspora' seeks to forge a unified identity among them and invokes common myths of origin. Further, in the new economic regime of liberalization in India, the Indian government, eager for investments from non-resident Indians (NRIs) as well as Indians abroad, is seeking to create a favourable atmosphere by speaking of the transnational Indian community as a unified, diasporic entity.

The Indian diaspora is smaller in size compared to the Jewish, African, Chinese and other diasporas, but is unique in many respects. It is spread over more than seventy countries and has made significant economic and political impact in at least twenty of those countries. Like its country of origin, the Indian diaspora is more culturally and socially varied than any other. In terms of class, diasporic Indians display ample class heterogeneity; they are engaged in occupations ranging from manual labour to entrepreneurial activity. Regional, linguistic, caste and religious variations from the countries of origin contribute to the diversity of the Indians abroad. For decades, overseas Indians had little or no contact with each other, contributing to vast differences in both their character as well as achievements (Parekh 1993). They followed distinct paths of development and acquired identities that were different from each other. For instance, the South African Indian immigrants were actively involved in anti-apartheid activities and Indians in Trinidad and Guyana were involved in creating a rich experiential literature. It was only after India's independence in 1947 that overseas Indians began to develop links both with the country of origin as well as with their counterparts in other countries. There is also the case of diasporic Indians moving from one part of the diaspora to another. The most common example of this kind of secondary migration has been that of the East African Indians emigrating to Britain and, in many instances, to the United States later on.

South Asians (a majority of whom are from India, with the rest being from Pakistan, Bangladesh, Sri Lanka, Nepal and Bhutan) have been scattered over many countries, especially across the English-speaking world. Indians have an ancient history of travelling abroad for trade and religious reasons. Buddhist pilgrims travelled to parts of Central and South Asia. The Palas of Bengal were in contact with the Sailendra empire in Indonesia. The ties with Indonesia continued under the Chola empire, but the impact of the Indians on the host culture was quite negligible. In 1902, Madho Singh, the Maharaja of Jaipur, attended the coronation of Edward VII, then Emperor of India, in London. Although the concept of migration was quite acceptable even in the Hindu epics (Rama leaving his kingdom to move south, and finally even cross the ocean), Madho Singh's visit to England across the Black Sea had to be carefully planned with the appropriate purification rituals.

This privileged visit abroad is, of course, quite different from the waves of Indian slaves who were 'exported' to different parts of the world, particularly to Central Asia, as early as the eleventh century (Kolff 1995). India was the main supplier of slaves until Iran took over in the seventeenth century. It was during the reign of the Mughal ruler, Shah Jahan that the exporting of 'Hindustan' slaves, a practice followed by the Turks, Afghans and the earlier Mughal rulers, was finally discontinued.

The Caribbean

After two decades of significant decline, a different form of imperialism started under the British rule. Many Indians went to different parts of the British empire during the nineteenth century when India was under British colonial rule. After the abolition of slavery in 1843, British colonial authorities needed cheap labour on their plantations and forced Indian workers to emigrate to other British colonies, like Mauritius, Guyana, the West Indies and Fiji. It was colonial rule with its economic reforms, such as new forms of land settlement and revenue collection, that made many peasants lose their lands to large landlords and money-lenders. The sense of homelessness accompanied landlessness and when migration became inescapable, emigration was not too much of a psychological obstacle.

Indians first arrived in Guyana to substitute for the newly-liberated African slaves and continued to come as indentured labourers until 1917. By 1911 Indians were the single largest ethnic group in Guyana (Ramnarine 1987). Between 1845 and 1916 approximately 37,000 Indians arrived in Jamaica as plantation labourers. Many of them worked for five-year contracts on the banana and sugarcane estates primarily in rural Jamaica on subsistence wages (Shepherd 1987). Gradually, as the Indians started seeking more remunerative employment, they started moving to urban Jamaica. By 1911, Indian migrants in urban Jamaica, composed mainly of time-expired and free Indians, were approximately six per cent of their total population. To Indians who had emigrated to far-off places, religion was a significant factor not only in maintaining ties with their homeland, but also a way in which they could orient their lives in an alien land. The hardships that they experienced on the plantations and the pressure from the Christian missionaries changed the complexion of religious activities among the immigrants. Jain (1993) compared the religious life of Indians in the Caribbean with that of Indians in Fiji. Christian missions in Trinidad and Guyana evinced keen interest in converting the immigrants. The Canadian Presbyterian Church in Trinidad, and the Presbyterians, Catholics and Anglicans in Guyana played a significant role in the religious life of the immigrants, even preaching in Bhojpuri and Hindi. However, by 1896 there was only one convert in Guyana, a number that went up only marginally in the later years. Hinduism, especially, in the form of the *Sanatana Dharma*, acted as a binding force cutting across caste boundaries. Jain comments on the process of Sankritization that took place in the early years, with many of the lower-caste Hindus in Trinidad, Guyana and Surinam giving up animal sacrifice and adopting the practices prescribed by the *Sanatana Dharma*.

Southeast Asia

Indians also migrated in large numbers to Southeast Asia to work as labourers and as clerical and administrative workers on the plantations. This heralded the era of out-migration for work which is continuing even to this day. There was a demand for labour from West Africa, Peru and Cuba along with the European colonies. Others, from the trader and merchant classes, left India in order to establish businesses in Mauritius, South Africa, and parts of eastern Africa in the late nineteenth and early twentieth centuries (Clark, Peach, and Vertovec 1990). Again, like their contemporaries in the Caribbean diaspora, most of the Indian labourers who signed up in Southeast Asia were single men and those who were married left their wives behind.

Exploitation of women who wanted to migrate, especially widows and wives, was quite intense and there were many broken families owing to the process of migration. The labourers were of two kinds, contract labour and indentured labour. Contract labourers, who were the ordinary form of wage labourers with their two-way passage paid and they were mostly from Tamil Nadu and Andhra Pradesh, went to Burma, Malaysia and Sri Lanka. The other, more common, form of labour, created by the British was indentured labour. The indentured labourer contracted himself for a fixed period of about five years and had to live on the plantation during that time. His mobility and activities were restricted and he was forbidden to work anywhere else. At the end of the contract period, he was sent back with a fully or a partially paid passage back to India. Most of the indentured labourers were Hindus from Bihar and Uttar Pradesh and they were in the fifteen British, French and Dutch colonies. Muslims and Sikhs formed a large proportion of the indentured labourers to East Africa (Parekh 1993). A large number of Sikhs were involved in the building of the Ugandan railway line as well as others in different parts of Southeast Asia.

Today, in Malaysia there are three major ethnic groups, the Indians, the Chinese and the Malays. The people who are lumped together as 'Indians' include the descendants of those who have been in the country for a century. They have inter-married with Chinese, speak the Malay language and have no ties with India. Low-caste Tamils who migrated during the colonial period and whose children continue to be labourers, and upper-caste Tamils and Malayalis who were in middle level supervisory positions in the colonial administration also constitute the Indians in the country. More than anything else, it is through religion that the Malaysian Indians have tried to maintain their identity (Mearns 1995).

South Africa

In South Africa, the Natal government passed a law in 1859 which made it possible for the British administration in India to export Indian labour. Initially, the British were reluctant as there were greater advantages for migrants to other colonies, but later on it could not stop the flow of labourers to South Africa. These labourers faced several problems, including abuse of their contracts. Further, they were sent to jails and asked to pay fines even if they complained about breaches of contract (Ginwala 1994). Towards the beginning of this century, traders as well as professionals, teachers, lawyers and priests, many of them Gujarati-speaking Hindus and Muslims, began to emigrate to South Africa.

Mohandas Gandhi, himself a lawyer from Gujarat, had begun a passive resistance movement against the government in 1905, initially against compulsory registration of individuals required by the Transvaal government. In 1913, he mobilized Indian workers in coal mines to fight against the injustices inflicted on the labourers. While several Indians participated in political activities against the apartheid regime, by joining organizations such as the African National Congress, deliberate government policies created a divide between the blacks and Indians. After decades of struggle, in 1962 Indians were acknowledged as a permanent part of the South African population. It was also in the 1960s that the Indians moved from largely agricultural occupations to industrial, manufacturing employment. This was a time when many Indians who were successful economically, began to collaborate with the South African government. This resulted in widening the gulf between the poorer Indians and blacks on the one hand, and between the poorer Indians and the more affluent Indians, on the other. With the abolition of apartheid, and the coming to power of a black-majority government led by Nelson Mandela in 1990, some prominent Indians gained cabinet positions. However, it should be expected that along with the process of national reconstruction with racial justice, there would also be a long period of reconciliation between the black population and the Indians. The activity of Indians in South Africa has been predominantly in the political sphere and it is only recently that reports of ethnic associations and religious groups have come into light.

Britain

Besides mostly forced migration to British colonies, a sizeable number of Indians have also gone directly to Britain for higher education and other purposes. Indians have been a substantial presence for well over half a century in Britain, which became one of the earliest sites for post-colonial struggles in economics, politics, literature, the arts, and religion. South Asians in Britain are mainly from India and Pakistan. Among the early Indians to go to Britain, were Sikhs, Muslims and Hindus. After World War II, there were still only about 7000 Asians in Britain but they increased more than a hundredfold in the next three decades (Tinker 1977). The greatest increase of Indian and Pakistani immigrants was in the 1960s. Sikhs started migrating with their families and, consequently, Sikh communities were formed and gurdwaras established in many parts of Britain. The first gurdwaras were started in Southall in 1962 and they have been increasing in number ever since. Many of the gurdwaras in Britain were first housed in nonconformist chapels which were abandoned with the waning of Christianity. Women have been involved in the organization of various activities in the gurdwaras. Sikhs have fought political and industrial battles to retain the right to wear their turbans and have often succeeded. Religion has been an important factor not only for the Sikhs but also for the Muslims from Pakistan, Bangladesh and India as well as for the Hindus, especially Gujaratis, in Britain. The Gujaratis have been one of the largest migratory groups from India and among them the Patels have emigrated in large numbers, first to East Africa and then to England and the United States.

Unlike the Asians in the United States, Indians in Britain are from various classes, engaged both in manual and clerical labour and in middle-class professional occupations. A number of people who have emigrated from agricultural occupations in Punjab and Gujarat were willing to take up low-paying jobs in England. Many women have also been involved in low-paying jobs in factories, laundries, and garment units. This concentration of a large number of South Asians in low-paying, working class occupations has resulted in a fairly conspicuous sense of solidarity with other coloured people, including the blacks. As constant victims of racial discrimination, the Indians and Pakistanis have been able, unlike in the United States, to forge links with other racial minorities. Many Indians in the diaspora, like the Gujarati immigrants in Uganda depicted in the 1992 movie, *Mississippi Masala*, experienced what can be called multiple displacements, having migrated from India to East Africa to Britain and finally to the United States.

The Gulf

Migration to West Asian countries, including the Persian Gulf, was negligible prior to 1950. In 1948, there were only 14,000 Indians spread over Aden, Bahrain, Egypt, Iran, Iraq, Kuwait, Muscat, Turkey, Jordan, Lebanon, Palestine, and Syria (Kondapi 1951). Since the 1970s, however, owing to the boom in oil and shortage of labour, there has been a rapid rise in Indians employed in the Gulf. There are currently 1.4 million Indians in the West Asian countries, of whom 1.3 million are in the Gulf (Jain 1994). The most significant motivation for Gulf migration is the high wages paid to the mostly male migrants who are engaged in unskilled or semi-skilled occupations. Women are often left behind to take care of the children and manage the large remittances that come from their spouses. Many of the Gulf migrants are from Kerala and have often faced problems of economic relocation on their return home. The impact of reinvestment by these migrants after they have moved up considerably in the socio-economic ladder is yet to be studied systematically. While the relatively more successful Gulf migrants tend to send their children to the United States for higher studies, others return home to face problems of economic reintegration. As most of the Gulf migration tends to be transitory and inspired largely by material considerations, there seems to be little motivation to establish cultural or religious institutions. Moreover, the political atmosphere of many of the Gulf countries precludes the possibility of institutionalizing alien religions.

ASIAN INDIANS[3] IN THE UNITED STATES

Indian immigration to the United States was intermittent until the mid-1960s. Prior to World War II, most of the Indian arrivals in America were Sikh farmers from the state of Punjab who settled in rural California and Canada. Since the past three decades, however, there has been a steady stream of Indian immigrants to the US, mostly from the urban, professional classes.

The Asian Indians in the United States are a unique group and an economically privileged lot in comparison to their counterparts in other parts of the world. It is this class advantage that enabled them to embellish their lives with religious institutions and activities. The very first record of an Asian Indian in America is that of a man who went from Madras to Salem, Massachusetts to expand trade between New England, Britain and South Asia. Indians did participate in California's Gold Rush of 1849, but the movements of people at that time were still quite sporadic. The arrival of Swami Vivekananda in 1893 is another landmark event which was celebrated a hundred years later by Indians in many parts of the United States.

The year 1901 marked the first significant immigration of the Sikhs from Punjab to the west coast of the United States. They

[3] The term 'Asian Indian' was created in the 1980 census for immigrants who came from India to the United States distinguishing them from 'American Indians' or Native Americans. In Great Britain the label 'East Indians' is used and in Africa it is just 'Asians'. Prior to 1980 'Asian Indian' was not a category but was part of an 'others' category. For scholarly purposes, however, the term South Asian has been used to include people living in the Indian subcontinent.

responded in large numbers to the call for 'hearty Punjabi Sikhs' to work on the Canadian Pacific Railways and migrated from Hong Kong to Vancouver and later moved to California. From railway work in Canada, many of these Sikhs took to agricultural labour in the United States. California had a scarcity of agricultural labour from the early nineteenth century and paid good wages to the agricultural labourers from Punjab (Jenson 1988). Between 1904 and 1923 their numbers might not have exceeded 6000. The reception given to them was quite cool and skeptical as they were following earlier Asian migrant labourers from Japan and China who were already being perceived as a threat to employment by the local population. These Punjabi farmers generally lived together in groups of about thirty, mainly for financial reasons. Some of these people returned to India in the 1920s when the US economy was worsening, but many stayed on permanently. In 1923, the US Supreme Court ruled that East Indians were not eligible for citizenship because they were not 'free white people' according to a 1790 naturalization law that restricted citizenship only to white people. This ruling had a direct impact on the demographic situation of Sikh migrants who were predominantly male. They sought Mexican brides as chances of finding Indians were quite low. This resulted in many of the Sikhs being identified with and assimilating into a Mexican-American culture. This process of assimilation, however, was not without its cultural tensions as the Mexican women were keen to raise children according to their own cultural values as opposed to the patriarchal values of their husbands. A study showed that almost twenty per cent of Mexican-Indian marriages in the Imperial Valley ended in divorce, which was a higher rate of divorce for an already divorce-prone California (Jenson 1988). Another reason for conflict in the family was the reallocation of financial resources. While the Sikh farmers wanted to use family income for buying or leasing more land in the valley, the women wanted to raise their standard of living. These older Sikh immigrants managed to preserve their religious practices, but not without changes in their traditions. Most of the men sported clean-shaven looks and got rid of their turbans. Sikhs who arrived on the shores of United States in later decades were to find themselves far more conservative than the older settlers.[4]

[4] In the 1970s, there was a growth in Sikh institutions across the United States and what started as informal gatherings in people's homes slowly turned

Apart from these rural migrants from Punjab there were a small cadre of students from India who had left to escape British colonialism. They faced discrimination even in the United States, but managed to organize themselves into supporting the freedom struggle in India. Gandhi was already in India after having fought racial discrimination in South Africa. The revolutionary or the *Ghadhar* party was formed in San Francisco and journals like *Free Hindustan* were started to express the views of the nationalist struggle in India. Americans were not very supportive of either the activities of the student leaders or of the Sikh agricultural labourers. Yet another Asian immigrant group in the White Man's land was subjected to the general orientalist attitudes. As far as American history books are concerned, the early immigrants from India are subsumed under larger groups such as the Japanese, Chinese and Mexican immigrants. The *Ghadhar* movement continued in the western United States, but on the east coast, the Home Rule League, a more moderate group had developed by 1910 and shaped by Lala Lajpat Rai, a member of the Indian National Congress in India, who became the leader of the League. The organization was further strengthened in the 1920s by revolutionary leaders such as Jayaprakash Narayan who was a student of the University of Wisconsin.

There was a constant debate over whether the Asian Indians should be allowed to get naturalized citizenship. The United States Immigration Service and the Asiatic Exclusions League (1907–13) classified the Indians as 'Oriental' and the discriminatory attitudes and practices that had already prevailed towards the Chinese and Japanese were extended to them. It was in 1926 that an Indian lawyer successfully argued that East Indians were Aryan, hence Caucasian (Helweg and Helweg 1990). The restrictive immigration laws against the Indians made them a target of American government attacks all through the 1930s. However,

---

into meetings in rented halls, and old churches were converted into full-fledged gurdwaras. Williams (1988) lists about fifty Sikh organizations spread over the United States. Their participation in the activities of other Indian groups declined in the 1980s with a large number of Sikhs interpreting the Indian army assault on the Golden Temple in Amritsar as a conflict between Hindus and Sikhs. The material as well as physical efforts which were put into building gurdwaras in the 1970s were converted into raising funds for riot victims in Punjab in the 1980s.

the tussle over citizenship rights continued until 1946 when the Roosevelt government successfully persuaded the Congress to pass a bill granting naturalization and providing an immigration quota for Indians. After India's independence in 1947, the Indian immigrants in the United States gained in self-confidence and a new sense of pride as people from free India in dealing with their problems with the American government. The first phase of the Indian immigrant experience in the United States culminated in the visit of Jawaharlal Nehru, the first Prime Minister of India, to the country in 1949 (Jensen 1988). The contributions of the Indian immigrants of the early phase, placed as they were either in self-employment, agriculture, or in the field of education, were rarely acknowledged by the American mainstream society. It was only the immigrants who came in the second half of the twentieth century, armed with the skills required for an advanced industrial economy, who attracted the host country's attention more directly.

Asian Indians emigrated to the United States in considerable numbers only after the Immigration Act of 1965 when, for the first time, a person's right to enter the United States did not depend on race. The primary policies of the Immigration Act of 1924 and the Nationality Act of 1952 (McCarran-Walter Act) had restricted the immigration of Asian Indians to the United States from 1890 to 1960 to 13,607 persons and resulted in the departure of some unrecorded number of people to India (Immigration and Naturalization Service 1982:2–4). These Acts assigned to different countries annual quotas based on national origin of the population of the United States in 1890, thus assuring the perpetuation of 'older immigrants' from northern and western Europe. While in the decade between 1951 and 1960 only 1973 persons emigrated from India to the US, as many as 22,607 Indians came in 1980 alone (Immigration and Naturalization Service 1982:6).

Census figures available for the year 1990 put the number of 'Asian Indians' in the United States at 815,447 (Gall and Gall 1993) which is less than one per cent of the total population of India. Like other immigrant groups, the Asian immigrants have been struggling to make themselves distinctive even as they undergo acculturation. Most of the Asian Indians in the United States today are first generation immigrants who are in the initial stages of drawing and maintaining their ethnic boundaries. According to an American Health Forum review in 1989, about seventy per cent of all Asian Indians in the United States were born in India (Gall and Gall 1993).

The 1990 census also shows that there has been a 110.6 per cent increase in the Asian Indian population of the United States from 387,223 in 1980 to 815,447 in 1990. Alongside this dramatic change in numbers, there was also a transformation in the educational and professional composition of the Indian immigrants. Those who left India since the sixties were primarily doctors, engineers, professors, and technicians (constituting the so-called 'brain drain') and their spouses and children. This was a result of President Lyndon Johnson's 1965 Act which showed a clear preference for the educated and professionals. Since the American economy was in the process of unprecedented expansion, many of the professional elites were offered jobs that were technically much more sophisticated and higher paying than in India (Bhardwaj and Rao 1990). Moreover, because of India's colonial past, most of its professionals were trained in English and, as a result, were easily incorporated into the American work force (Krauter and Davis 1978:93).

In 1975, ninety-three per cent of the Indians admitted were classified as 'professional/technical workers' or 'spouses and children of professional and technical workers' (Singh 1979:41). According to 1984 figures, about forty-three per cent of Asian Indians (male and female) were professionals; about eighty-nine per cent of them (male and female) were at least high school graduates of whom about sixty-six per cent were college graduates. The median household income of Indians living in the United States was estimated to be at $25,644 in 1984. This income level can to a great extent be attributed to the fact that about fifty-five per cent of all Indian women over sixteen years of age are in the labour force. Despite this degree of comfort and relative affluence, Indian immigrants to the United States, like immigrants to other places, have had to face an epistemological crisis related to their identities as well as to the cultural gaps between the home country and the host country.

The epistemological crisis experienced by immigrants tends to be quite varied along lines of gender, ethnicity, class, religion, and language even within a single immigrant group. Writings on the immigrant experience, however, have generally tended to treat the 'immigrant' as a monolithic construct. Gender, for example, has not been a significant analytic category in a number of studies about immigrants. Nevertheless, the gender dimension is particularly significant as the experience of the crisis as well as attempted resolutions to it are both gendered. Immigrant women's experiences cannot be treated as if they are identical to men's as their very reasons for entering the alien society and culture may be different from those of men. Some women emigrate for their own independent reasons, but many accompany their fathers or husbands. The consequences of this kind of 'dependent immigration' can perhaps be seen in the new society in the perpetuation of traditional gender roles within social institutions such as the family and religion.[5]

A major symbolic resource used by many immigrants in the rebuilding of community is religion. Religion provides a powerful means to preserve and reinforce group identity. In the United States, religion has been associated with societal difference and it is common for immigrants to become conscious of their distinctive religious identity in a pluralistic society (Warner 1993a). In a culturally plural society which encourages devout citizens, religion becomes a central identity factor for immigrants. For Indian immigrants, as for others, religion is one of the identity markers that helps them preserve their individual self-awareness and group cohesion. This need to remain distinctive may motivate immigrants to be more religiously active than they were in their home country and heightens their religious consciousness (Williams 1988:11). This heightened religiosity can be evidenced in the construction of numerous temples in different parts of the Indian diaspora, including the United States.

Hindu temples in North America may be categorized into four main types: the Hare Krishna temples; sectarian temples such as those of the Swaminarayan sect or of Sai Baba; temples with a north Indian orientation; and those with a south Indian orientation

[5] Most of the South Indian women in my study were not like Smith's (1980:79–80) Portuguese immigrant women — 'the pushers, the naggers, the needlers, the schemers, the manipulators, the innovators'. I do not, however, wish to perpetuate the image of immigrant women as 'passive followers' which has often led to neglecting their roles in the new society. I would like to emphasize that the literature tends to underplay the significance of female immigrants and treat 'their role . . . as limited, trivial and inconsequential' (Smith 1980:80).

(Bhardwaj 1991). Major Hindu temples in the United States with a predominantly south Indian orientation include Venkateswara temples at Pittsburgh (the site of my research), Chicago, and Los Angeles, the Shiva Vishnu temple near San Francisco, the Meenakshi temple at Houston, and the Ganesh Temple in New York.

Studies conducted among Indian immigrants have shown that there are gender differences in religious behaviour, indicating that more women than men participate in religious activities (e.g. Ghosh 1983; Clothey 1983). Research on religion and gender roles has mainly been based on the assumption that women are more religious than men or that, at least, there are gender differences in the ways in which men and women practice religion (Hargrove 1985). Women all over the world have always played an important role in the transmission and perpetuation of tradition and culture. In most religious traditions it is the women who perform and organize religious rituals within the family (Haddad and Findly 1985; Falk and Gross 1989). Hinduism, like many other religions, has been instrumental in legitimizing a patriarchal order, but women are known to be quite involved in the religious and ritual sphere (Robinson 1985). Among some Hindus, women play a prominent role in the observance of rituals at home, but they are not active in the public realm (Srinivas 1978; Hanchett 1988; Wadley 1989; Jacobson 1989).[6] In this study I show how South Indian immigrants at the Sri Venkateswara (S.V.) temple in Pittsburgh, the primary site of my research, negotiate this boundary between women's roles in the domestic and public spheres.

IMMIGRANT WOMAN AS AN ANALYTIC CONSTRUCT

A review of the literature on immigrant groups reveals that women have been left out of many studies, as is the case in other areas of social science research in which women's experiences have generally been subsumed under those of men (Jacobson 1979). As Dumon (1981) points out, women have been treated as 'migrants' wives' rather than as 'female migrants', and their roles have been relegated to those of less important followers.

---

[6] Although all these anthropological studies are based on fieldwork in rural India, the situation in the urban areas is not very different.

Gerda Lerner (1979) suggested that one could include women in history in three different ways — 'contributions' history (adding women to the text by examining their contributions in conventionally male domains), 'women-centred' history (focusing on women's unique experiences), and 'gender-integrated' history (the synthesis of both male and female experiences). Feminist historians of immigration and ethnicity have only recently begun the process of writing a gender-integrated history. Maxine Schwartz Seller (1992) advocates pursuing all three modes of inquiry simultaneously. These three modes of investigating women's experiences are also applicable to fields other than history, such as sociology and anthropology. I attempt, in my study, to mainly combine the 'women-centred' and 'gender-integrated' approaches to analyse the experiences of South Indian Hindus in Pittsburgh.

Studies of immigrant groups that include women focus on those aspects of life that most resemble men's — e.g. wage labour. One reason for the marginalization of immigrant women in community studies is that the 'uniquely female or private familial events' are considered less important by scholars studying immigrant lives (Gabaccia 1991:64). Further, one needs to be cautious about treating immigrants in terms of homogeneous nationality constructs and, instead, recognize heterogeneity and difference. For example, treating 'the African immigrant' as if it were a single homogeneous category masks vast differences in terms of country, ethnicity, and class.

Efforts to rectify this omission in the immigration literature have begun only in the early 1980s as scholars have come to assert that 'birds of passage are also women' (Morokvasic 1984).[7] More recent studies, including the articles published in the special issue of *International Migration Review* (1984), those in the volume edited by Simon and Brettell (1986), and the 'cross-cultural perspectives on women and immigration' presented by Browner and King (1989), show us that immigrant women's experiences are unique and sometimes quite different from those of their male counterparts.

[7] The journal, *International Migration Review*, published only five studies on women migrants from 1964 through the early 1980s. It was only in 1984 that a whole issue was dedicated to women migrants and their role in the processes of national and international migration. Most of the articles in this special issue dealt with women's participation in the labour market or with demographic changes among the immigrant population.

A sizeable minority of female immigrants to the US from Europe in the late nineteenth and early twentieth centuries came on their own initiative (Seller 1981). Yet for many of them immigration was an extension of the traditional role of the dutiful daughter as they sent money to family and siblings back home. Women who moved from rural Europe to industrial Pittsburgh often sought strength and support from their churches, their neighbours, their ethnic communities and their families (Krause 1978). However, with these few exceptions, most studies primarily explore immigrant women's economic contributions, giving less importance to cultural issues.

While many studies document changes in immigrant women's lives, at least marginally, they do not place gender roles in a meaningful context. Sydney Stahl Weinberg (1992), in a review essay on immigrant women in history, points out that what has been left unexamined in many of these studies are

what women thought of their own authority, their attitudes toward acculturation, changes in women's status between the old country and new, and perhaps even significant differences between the attitudes of first generation men and women. . . . Thus we do not learn about the texture of women's lives: how did they see themselves, socialize their children, participate in neighbourhood life, maintain kinship relationships, establish sex-linked ties and create their own sense of values and neighbourhood? (Weinberg 1992:33–4).

I also examine, as Weinberg urges researchers to do, the connections between domestic and public spheres, arguing that the Hindu immigrants in Pittsburgh renegotiate these spheres as well as the roles of men and women within those domains (see chapter IV).

Sarah Deutsch (1987), in her historical study of Hispanic immigrants in southwestern United States, reassesses the role played by ethnic women in the maintenance or transformation of culture. Hispanic women, much more than men, were responsible for building social networks that helped to ensure the smooth functioning of the community. Similarly, in one of the more instructive anthropological studies about gender relations among ethnic groups, Micaela di Leonardo (1987) focused upon the way Italian-American women engage in 'kin work' within their community. Deutsch's study and, in a more significant way, Leonardo's exploration of the links between work and home are useful in understanding the nature of community building among South

Indians in Pittsburgh. The women immigrants in Pittsburgh, like the Italians in Leonardo's study, seem to draw emotional fulfilment and autonomous power from their work in establishing and maintaining community networks.

Thus, although there is an emerging recognition of immigrant women's lives, few studies investigate the links between religion and women's experiences in the immigrant context. My study of South Indian immigrant women in Pittsburgh analyses women's lives in a religious setting, the S.V. temple.

IMMIGRANT WOMEN AND RELIGION

Religion is a key element in the lives of many immigrants. It is common among immigrant groups to engage in identity-formation through religious expression. McLellan's study of the role of religion in the lives of Tibetan Buddhist immigrants in Ontario, Canada, shows how 'religion has provided the main avenue for structural relationships, not only giving individuals a relevant series of linkages to each other, but forming the primary basis for expressing and mobilizing their generalized "ethnic identity"' (McLellan 1987:64). Similarly, for the Hindu immigrants in the United States, religion forms the context within which they seek to maintain their identity and also socialize their children (Williams 1988).

Women in many cultures have used their religion and ethnic background to maintain a distinctiveness in the immigrant context. It is possible, of course, that religion and ethnicity may not have an equal and uniform effect on identity-formation for all immigrant groups in all contexts. For instance, in the case of Ethiopians in Israel, where Judaism is the overwhelming presence, religion does not seem to be as instrumental as their 'Ethiopianness' in maintaining their distinctive identity (Doleve-Gandelman 1990). Ethiopian Jewish women in Israel retain traditional cooking methods and engage in other practices that help them sustain their ethnic identity in the new Israeli culture.

On the other hand, many Muslim women immigrants (from Morocco and Turkey) in the Netherlands experience greater awareness of being Muslim and have a greater need for acquiring more knowledge about Islam than they had felt in their home countries (Speelman 1988). Algerian female immigrants in France

(Andezian 1986), similarly, take an active part in maintaining and expanding religious practices, as well as in creating a new symbolic order within the community. These Algerian Islamic women are more actively religious in France than they were in their home country. Palestinian women in the United States also do a vast majority of the culture preservation work, making concerted efforts not to 'become Americanized' (Cainkar 1988).

Lagerquist's (1991) study about Norwegian immigrants in the United States, from the turn of the century to the present, focuses on the influences of gender, ethnicity, and religion on the Americanization of Norwegian-American women. These variables — gender, ethnicity and religion — are also central to my study on Hindu immigrants in Pittsburgh. However, my study does not include three generations of immigrants (as Lagerquist's does), but instead examines the experiences of first-generation Indian immigrants who constitute more than seventy per cent of the total Asian Indian population in the United States.

WOMEN IN THE ASIAN INDIAN DIASPORA

Gender has not been problematized in a central way by scholars studying immigrants, and the experiences of Asian Indian women have not been adequately represented in the writings on immigrants. Women have been accorded only a small part in larger research projects about Asian Indians in the United States (e.g. Fisher 1980; Saran 1985; Helweg and Helweg 1990). There are few significant studies focusing on Asian Indian women in the United States.[8] In the works of Clothey (1983), Fenton (1988), Williams (1988), and Helweg and Helweg (1990) which examine Indian immigrants' religious lives, there are references to women, but gender is not the central focus. There is little work on the women among the first phase of Indian immigrants in the US, partly because of their negligible numbers. The sex ratio of Indians in the US, like in other parts of the diaspora, during that period was such that most men either arrived single or left their wives behind.

[8] Josephine Naidoo's (1980:51) assertion that 'empirical studies on women of non-western origin living on the North American continent are virtually non-existent except as larger surveys of ethnic minorities' needs to be qualified as there have been in the last decade some studies on the subject mentioned later in this chapter.

For instance, in the Caribbean, the sex ratio of Indians was quite skewed because women's emigration was constrained by caste, the joint-family system and other socio-cultural factors. In Guyana, the sex ratio in 1857 was thirty-five women to a hundred men which progressively rose to 50:100 by 1860. Among those who left India were prostitutes, young widows or other women who were keen on escaping the patriarchal clutches of their families. Indians in Guyana also faced a legal dilemma since the government refused to recognize marriages performed outside Guyana. The disproportionate sex ratio accompanied by non-recognition of traditional marriages created problems such as a high number of wife murders and other acts of violence against Indian women in Guyana as well as other colonies (Mangru 1987). There was also a public slandering of the character of Indian women by projecting acts of polyandry as sexual immorality on the part of the women.

. . . the experience of Indian women during the indenture period was one of multiple oppression: as an indentured worker in a system of quasi-servitude, as an Indian whose culture was despised as barbaric and heathen by all other sections of the population, and as a woman who suffered from the sexual depredations of the white overseer class and was restricted within the 'Indian' family structure (Poynting 1987:231–2).

The imbalance in the sex ratio also led to child marriages and discrimination of young married women in the spheres of education and other benefits. It was only in the 1950s when attitudes toward education began to change, especially in Trinidad, when the Hindu Maha Sabha, the Arya Samaj, and Islamic organizations built denominational schools for both girls and boys. On the economic front, women began to work in the urban consumer economy which saw a major boom in the 1960s and 1970s. In Trinidad's rural areas and in Guyana, they were part of the agricultural labourers who earned far less than their male counterparts.

In the US, by 1984 the sex ratio of Asian Indians was estimated to be one hundred and twenty-four men for a hundred women (Helweg and Helweg 1990). Most of these women had accompanied their husbands or fathers to the US, but once they did that they have not only played a critical role in the socialization of children and maintenance of traditions, but also assumed a major financial responsibility in the household. In spite of this centrality of women, their contributions to the construction of an Indian community in the US have not been adequately recognized by scholars.

However, in the past few years there have been more studies emerging from diasporic scholars, mostly in cultural studies, that discuss gender issues in the construction of Indian immigrant identities. Keya Ganguly's (1992) study about Bengali immigrants' construction of selfhood in New Jersey focuses on how post-coloniality as well as the immigrant condition influences men and women differently. Ganguly shows how her respondents engage in the reinvention of the past in ways which are specific to the 'gendering of experience'. I examine a similar gendering of experiences in my analysis of the gender ideologies and strategies of the Indian immigrants in Pittsburgh.

In her book about Indians in New Jersey, Sathi Dasgupta (1989) devoted a chapter on the changing roles of women. She found that since most of the Indian immigrant women in her study feel a loss of social networks and are isolated in the US, they gain little in terms of status when compared to the losses they experience. My study challenges this notion of a complete loss of social networks, since the Indian immigrant women in Pittsburgh feel empowered precisely in building networks on their own, without the constraints of the extended family in India.

However, Indian women often serve as the transmitters of tradition and the immigrant women take on this mantle. In her article on the 'Indian immigrant bourgeoisie' and the construction of 'Indianness', Anannya Bhattacharjee (1992) critically examines the way in which the immigrant community creates a model of a woman who is a representative of the pure 'nation'. She says that the construction of woman is always 'pure', in the image of ancient Hindu goddesses, and there is a systematic indifference toward anything that challenges the prototype of the Indian woman. Issues such as domestic violence and lesbianism are, often, therefore, ignored by the Indian immigrants.[9]

There are a few social psychological studies that shed light on changes that Indian immigrants to US and Canada go through after their arrival. Uma Segal (1991) explores the cultural values

---

[9] South Asian women's groups in larger cities, such as New York, have begun to deal with issues such as domestic violence. There are no such groups in Pittsburgh yet and problems such as domestic violence have not come out in the open even if they exist.

of Asian Indians and analyses the problems of acculturation. Unfortunately, some of the domestic violence cases are often written off as part of the larger process of the immigrant male's psychological adjustment. While she focuses on changes associated with the joint (extended) family structure to the nuclear family structure, she does not discuss gender issues related to the shifting family structure.

In another study from the social psychological perspective, Shamita Das Dasgupta (1986) measured the relationship between Indian immigrant women's sex roles and their occupational roles. Dasgupta found that there was no great difference in sex role ideology between homemakers and women who work outside the home. Some of Dasgupta's findings were supported in my study, especially with regard to gender role socialization of children. Dasgupta cursorily points out that there are some gaps in sex role attitudes and behaviour of Indian women. I seek to show how the South Indians in my study attempt to reconcile the gaps that exist between their gender ideology and practice. Since Dasgupta's study is psychologically oriented, there is a concentration on attitudinal and behavioural patterns and less of an emphasis on the influence of social networks.

Female Indian immigrants in Canada and Britain have certainly received greater attention from scholars than their counterparts in the US. Many of the studies on Asian Indian women in those countries focused on immigrant women in the labour market (Wilson 1978; Arnopoulos 1979; Silvera 1981; Ng 1981, 1986; Bhachu 1986).[10] Amrit Wilson's (1978) book on Asian women's lives in Britain, for example, while providing a fascinating experiential account, concentrated mostly on immigrant women workers caught between two different cultures. Religion and larger questions of culture were not accorded importance.

A number of Canadian studies dealt with women and ethnic issues or the problem of identity in an alien culture, reflecting governmental concerns about multiculturalism (Ghosh 1981a,

---

[10] While many of the Indian women in the United States are engaged in middle-class occupations, Indian immigrants, women as well as men, in Canada and Britain have had, as already discussed above, a harder life in working class occupations. This reflects the social class differences between the early immigrants to the British Commonwealth and the later (and more recent) ones to the United States.

1981b, 1983; Naidoo 1985a, 1985b; Dasgupta 1986). Ratna Ghosh (1981a, 1983) pointed out that maintenance of cultural identity is an important concern for Indian women in Canada and they, more than men, are 'custodians of religious and cultural convictions'. However, this cultural role does not mean that these women are largely 'traditional' in their value system. Naidoo and Davis (1988) asserted that ideologically, the Indian women in their study are more complex, shifting their perspectives from 'traditional' to 'contemporary' depending on the particular social or cultural issue.

Helen Ralston (1988) explored the dynamics of ethnicity, class, and gender as experienced by South Asian women in Metro Halifax, Canada. This study was useful as a preliminary guide to research among the Indians in Pittsburgh. The experiences of the South Asian women were examined in the domestic sphere, in the labour market, and in the social and religious spheres. Ralston found that gender relations inside and outside the home gave women the responsibility of maintaining ethnic identity for themselves and their children through everyday religious, cultural, and social activities. Since most of these women had arranged marriages they had 'theoretically agreed to the man's control over gender relations' and accepted culturally defined gender roles including the responsibility for transmission of culture (Ralston 1988:71). Most of the Indian immigrants in my study in Pittsburgh had arranged marriages as well, but this certainly does not mean that men automatically have control over the women.

In a survey on ethnic cultural retention among first generation Hindu immigrants in Canada, Vanaja Dhruvarajan (1993) compares the gender ideologies of men and women, using such variables as religiosity, occupation, education, and length of stay in Canada. She found that the patriarchal values that the Indian immigrants brought with them from India are perpetuated to a considerable extent in the Canadian context. Religiosity is also a relevant dimension in my study as my sample in Pittsburgh is restricted to those who frequent the S.V. temple.

ASIAN INDIANS IN PITTSBURGH

Most of the Indian immigrants in the United States are clustered in major metropolitan areas such as New York, New Jersey, Washington DC, Chicago, Houston, and Los Angeles. Pennsylvania, which is among the states with a sizeable population of Indian immigrants, has, according to the 1990 census, about 28,396 Indians. About 4618 of those Indians who made Pennsylvania their home live in the Pittsburgh Consolidated Metropolitan Statistical Area which has a total population of 2,242,730. As the largest Asian group in Pittsburgh, Asian Indians constitute about 29.27 per cent of the total Asian population in the city.

Although areas such as New York City and Los Angeles have a far greater number of Indians, Pittsburgh has gained in importance primarily because of the establishment of the Sri Venkateswara temple by South Indian Hindus in the city. Many of the Indian immigrants in Pittsburgh were attracted to the city because of its academic and industrial opportunities (Clothey 1983). The Indian immigrants in Pittsburgh are highly educated and 75.2 per cent of the entire sample population in Clothey's 1978 study had a graduate degree, including 86.3 per cent of the men and 54.9 per cent of the women (Clothey 1983).

The Indians in Pittsburgh have different religious affiliations as do Indians anywhere in the world. In Clothey's study, 81.2 per cent of the population surveyed were Hindu, 5.4 per cent were Sikh, five per cent were Jain, 2.5 per cent Muslim and two per cent Christian. Although a majority of the Pittsburgh Indians are Hindus, differences in regional and linguistic affiliations shape variations in forms of worship. This partly explains the fact that there are two Hindu temples in Pittsburgh, one Hindu-Jain temple which is frequented mostly by North Indian Hindus and Jains, and the other, Sri Venkateswara temple which is frequented mostly by South Indians in Pittsburgh and Hindus from various parts of northeastern and midwestern US and southeastern Canada. There is a Sikh gurdwara in Pittsburgh as well as a South Asian Islamic Centre. It is significant that all the religious institutions of South Asian origin are found in the suburbs of Monroeville in East Pittsburgh. Indian immigrants are not known for forming exclusive geographical spaces like Chinatowns or Little Italys, but have established their presence in the professional, upper middle class American suburbia. Sikhs in Pittsburgh are not a particularly visible group but they do have their pockets of influence in different parts of the Greater Pittsburgh area. They are different from the Sikhs in California, and more like the professionals who migrated to England and Canada after 1960. The Indian Muslims who live in Pittsburgh are in the process of institutionalizing their community centre. They do not participate in the activities of the mosques which are run by people of Middle eastern origin, but they interact more with other South Asian Muslims from Bangladesh and Pakistan. During this interaction with other South Asian groups, women's roles get transformed and the Muslim women from India have had to adapt to certain traditions that have been borrowed from Pakistan.

THE BIRTH OF A TEMPLE

Inaugurated in 1977, the S.V. temple is located in the Penn Hills area in Pittsburgh. It has a fascinating history and is the product of committed efforts by some immigrant Indians to recreate their cultural traditions and heritage in an alien land.[11] A group of Indians in Pittsburgh who were a part of the India Association had been meeting irregularly for some time for religious and social activities. The impetus for some kind of institutionalization of these activities came from a performance of *Bharata Natyam*, a classical dance form of southern India, in December 1971 at the University of Pittsburgh. A South Indian couple Rajni and Ram Krishna[12] who were in the audience were so impressed that they wanted their daughters and other Indian girls in Pittsburgh to learn this 'divine art'.

This desire to transmit Indian culture and heritage resulted in a regular dance class for some twenty girls in the Pittsburgh area. They began these classes in a basement of an Indian businessman's store in Squirrel Hill in Pittsburgh, where they met every Sunday. The adults then created a small shrine there so that the children could pray before beginning their class. That was when Rajni Krishna said she began to dream of a 'real' temple and was displeased about housing Hindu gods in a basement instead of 'on a river bed or mountain top' as is traditionally done.

---

[11] For a detailed history of the Sri Venkateswara (S.V.) Temple in Pittsburgh, see Clothey (1983). For the description of the temple and its various activities, see chapter II of my study.

[12] I have used pseudonyms throughout this study to protect my respondents' privacy. Rajni Krishna was one of my respondents who gave a detailed account of the history of the temple. I will discuss the crucial role played by women in the establishment of the temple in chapter IV.

Funds were raised among the Indians in the Pittsburgh area and contact was established with those in New York who were planning to build the Ganesha temple with the assistance of a temple foundation, the Tirumala Tirupati Devasthanam (TTD) in India.[13] The Hindu Temple Society of North America was thus set up in 1973 as an affiliate of the New York organization, and land was purchased along with a church building in Murraysville which is now the Hindu-Jain temple. However, over the next three years there was a 'big split' caused by the resignations of some key members from the organization due to differences over the issue of presiding deities. The Sri Venkateswara temples that are funded by the TTD follow the *Vaishnava* tradition of Hinduism and do not house Shaivite deities. The Hindu-Jain temple that was later established in Murraysville, about four miles away from the S.V. temple, has deities from both traditions.

The root causes of this split lie, perhaps, in the historical primacy of temples in south India and the differences in temple cultures of north and south India. Medieval South Indian temples played a major role as agents of control of the state's economic resources by instituting irrigation projects and other works that were useful for the people (Stein 1961). The temple as a religious institution had functions that were far-reaching in the economic, political and administrative spheres. Similarly the rajas in south India were actively engaged in creating a centralized temple structure that formed the identity of the presiding deity as well as the temple itself. The Tirumala Tirupati Devasthanam inherited the above principles of centralized rituals as well as involvement in several social, cultural, economic and educational activities. The Tirumala temple has for decades held a central place in south Indian religious activity. There has been no temple in the north which has the same pull for north Indians as the Sri Venkateswara temple in Tirupati has for South Indians.[14] It is this culturally inherited experience of the South Indian tradition backed strongly

---

[13] The TTD has offices in many parts of the world to organize pilgrimages to the Tirupati temple and promote Hinduism. They also have programmes to assist building of temples in the United States and elsewhere.

[14] It is only with the recent resurgence of Hindu fundamentalism that places like Ayodhya and Mathura have been accorded a great deal of importance by the Bharatiya Janata Party and the Vishwa Hindu Parishad which have the avowed aim of creating a Hindu religious site in North India, parallel to the Mecca or the Vatican.

by the financial and religious support from Tirupati that has made it possible for the establishment of South Indian temples in the Indian diaspora.

After the split among the Pittsburgh Indian immigrants, the South Indians decided to continue with the TTD funding and build a Venkateswara temple, then began to look for an alternative site. About one hundred and twenty sculptors had already begun work in Tirupati for the temple in Pittsburgh. While driving by Penn Hills, the Krishnas saw land for sale which reminded them of the Tirupati Hills. The land was soon purchased and the temple built with the assistance of skilled temple architects and craftsmen from India. The compelling force of tradition over these pioneering men and women can be seen in their missionary zeal and the dedication with which they accomplished the task.

The S.V. temple, officially dedicated in June 1977, is today the largest, wealthiest (an income of approximately $1 million a year) and one of the most successful Hindu temples outside India. It has become a major pilgrimage centre for thousands of immigrant Indians on the east coast and in the midwest of the United States. The presiding deity in the temple, Lord Venkateswara, is believed by millions in south India to be the most benevolent one, fulfilling the wishes of devotees. In a study of donors to the S.V. temple, Bhardwaj and Rinschede (1988) point out that the Pittsburgh deity has become a favourite among many Hindus, as reflected in the large donations received by the temple. The S.V. temple in Pittsburgh is also strategically located as there are not many other temples in the area that compete for donations. Apart from the Hindu-Jain temple, the other big temple to the east of Pittsburgh is the Ganesha temple in Flushing, New York and in the west are the Rama and Balaji Temples in Chicago. According to the Bhardwaj and Rinschede study, the S.V. temple's donorship is mostly of South Indian origin (about eighty per cent). This study also showed that the median distance travelled by the pilgrims to the temple was three hundred miles and the median frequency of visits was three times in a calendar year. These visits by pilgrims from outside Pittsburgh are usually organized during major US holidays like Memorial Day, Independence Day, and Labour Day.

A 1962 *Report of the Hindu Religious Endowments Commission* stressed that Hindu temples in south India are not merely centres of religion, but also serve as active repositories and transmitters

of the many institutions of Hindu culture (Bhardwaj and Rinschede 1988:177). Hindu temples in the United States and other
parts of the world are continuing a similar tradition, raising significant social and cultural issues in the immigrant context.

In an informative article on identity issues among Indian
immigrants in Canada, Paranjpe (1986) showed how the establishment of religious institutions has been one of the main pre-
occupations of the Indians in the last few decades. Indo-Canadians
in Vancouver have set up businesses, entered politics, and built
temples, gurdwaras, and mosques. While Paranjpe found that
Indian immigrants in Canada were initially more concerned about
their success in the workplace, resulting in the neglect of religion,
in Pittsburgh religious socialization of children has been a vital
goal from the early 1970s, even before the construction of the
temple. This difference could perhaps be explained by the different class composition of Indian immigrants in Canada and the
US. Many Indians in the US are of an upper-middle class background, while those in Canada are a mixed group with a number
of people in working class occupations. The former have greater
resources for religious socialization and their relative economic
security permitted them to accord a high priority to the establishment of a temple.

The people who frequent the temple are mostly those of South
Indian origin (mainly people from the four southern states —
Karnataka, Tamil Nadu, Andhra Pradesh and Kerala) in the
Greater Pittsburgh area. People from these states speak different
languages — Kannada, Tamil, Telugu, and Malayalam, respectively — and have some differences in their religious rituals and
practices. However, there are visitors from other Indian states as
well. The chanting of hymns is in Sanskrit and the priests speak
all four South Indian languages as well as English and Hindi to
communicate with the devotees. The multi-lingual culture of
Indians made it possible for me to approach people even if I did
not understand their mother tongue.

My case study of South Indian Hindu immigrants in Pittsburgh
is what is conventionally seen as a 'microsociological'[15] attempt to

[15] Robertson (1994), in his discussion of the relationship between the 'global'
and the 'local', points out that the former cannot be conceptualized as a
supra-entity that does not include the local. He extends the same critique to

understand how one displaced group combined their memories of place and religion to imaginatively reconstruct a new community[16] in what is increasingly being talked about as a diaspora.

OVERVIEW

In this book, I attempt to understand the process in which an 'imagined community' is being reconstructed in an immigrant context. While mapping the contours of this imagined community as it currently exists, I explore the complex dynamics of gender roles and relations among its members. I focus especially on the different ways in which the women have created a niche for themselves within the community, challenging conventional notions of gender roles and behaviour.

I examine the way these middle and upper-middle class immigrants have constructed an imagined world in an alien land by combining old-world values with new contingencies in the US. The S.V. temple is a symbol of the contributions of Hindu immigrants to the cultural plurality of the US. Other studies have emphasized the salience of religion for Indian immigrants, but few have focused on gender issues. It is this intersection of religion and gender, as it is lived out in the lives of Hindu immigrants in the US, especially in women's lives, that I examine here. In Pittsburgh, particularly, the South Indian women play a crucial role not only in the transmission of culture to the second generation but also in the formal organization of one of the largest temples outside India.

In the past decade research on the roles of immigrant women in community life has been on the rise. However, while there is a recognition that gender as a category is cross-cut by other factors such as race, religion, and ethnicity, there are only a few analyses of whether and how immigrant women's lives are influenced by religion. My examination of Hindu women's experiences in this study attempts such an analysis. This is a story of women who

---

the macro-micro distinction in social sciences. The usage of the term 'micro-sociology' in my work is, thus, informed by that critique.

16 I use 'community' in this work mainly as a descriptive term for the immigrants in my study. I do not use it as a construct that posits an 'ontically secure' home against the homogenizing wave of 'globalization', a tendency Robertson (1994) cautions against.

played a pioneering role in the construction and maintenance of the temple as well as of those who take the lead in the reproduction and recreation of culture for their community.

I analyse issues such as gender, ethnicity, religion, and class in an immigrant context. I show that, through a complex set of gender dynamics, the Indian immigrant women in Pittsburgh challenge conventional notions of separate and distinct public and private spheres. In order to do that I draw upon feminist discourses on the overlapping of public and private spheres. Numerous feminist studies have discussed this overlapping by bringing to light women's roles in the workplace. However, my study characterizes the S.V. temple as the site of such an intersection (of the public and the private) by exploring women's roles in both the rational, bureaucratic arenas of the temple as well as in the more private tasks of socialization of children.

An interesting question for the study was whether the performance of rational, bureaucratic functions at the temple by women suggests a post-immigration transition to a broader, egalitarian ideology and practice among the Indian immigrants. I seek an answer to this question by analysing the gender ideologies and strategies of the Indian immigrants in Pittsburgh not only at the temple but also with regard to gender roles at home. I show that gender ideologies tend to vary in different aspects of life and that gender strategies may not necessarily coincide with ideologies espoused by the immigrants.

The new world for immigrants, involving significant epistemological transformations, is quite different from the one they were a part of back home. Gender ideologies and practices change as part of a dialectical process of accommodation and resistance to the new cultural milieu. I provide a 'thick description' of the rich texture of women's lives and explore how existing gender relations are sustained as well as transformed within the Indian diaspora. Although this ethnographic study is mainly a sociological narrative of the experiences of Indian women in Pittsburgh, it can illuminate more general social and cultural trends among the so-called new immigrant groups.

In chapter II, I describe the ethnographic method I have used in this study, involving participant observation and interviews with women and men in the community. I also explain the qualitative analysis techniques I have used to make sense of the data. Finally, this chapter also includes a reflexive account of my experiences as a researcher and of the insider/outsider dilemmas I encountered during my research in fieldwork.

In chapter III, I examine the various ways in which South Indian immigrant women attempt to adhere to the values of their country of origin while at the same time adapting and accommodating some of the cultural features of the host country. I show how the nostalgia that they experience as part of being away from home finds expression in the celebration of community at the temple. I explore the cultural practices of the immigrants while focusing on the ways in which these practices contribute to the perpetuation and reconstruction of gender relations among them. There are different levels of identity that come into play within the larger diasporic identity and I analyse the ways in which the Hindu immigrants deal with these layers of identity and show the importance accorded to gender identity by the women.

In chapter IV, I delineate how Hindu immigrants in Pittsburgh constructed a local temple as an intersection of the private and public worlds. I contend that a complex set of gender dynamics confront and break down the dichotomy between these apparently separate arenas. In order to do this, I draw upon feminist theoretical discourses that challenge the dichotomization of public and private spheres as typically male and female arenas. On the one hand, the S.V. temple is a symbol of these new immigrants' public assertion of their presence in a 'multicultural' society. On the other hand, a temple community, as the one in Pittsburgh, serves as a surrogate extended family for the women, men, and their children who frequent it. Women are highly visible in the public aspects of the temple by taking part in its formal, bureaucratic structure, while, at the same time, taking an active role in the socialization of their American-born offspring, a task that is said to be relegated to the private realm of the family. I examine how different levels of the public/private realms are re-negotiated by the Indian immigrant women and men in the temple as well as in other aspects of their lives.

In chapter V, I use the analytical framework borrowed from Arlie Hochschild (1989) to investigate the varied gender ideologies that co-exist among the women and men in my study and attempt to relate these ideologies to actual practices. I compare the status of Indian women before and after immigration, drawing on relevant literature as well as on my own data on different aspects of immigrant lives. I trace the cultural representations of the 'ideal' Hindu woman, first by examining mythological constructs of the role of women, and then by providing some empirical data on contemporary values and attitudes about gender issues in India. In this context, I examine the role of the mass media in fostering or reinforcing the larger cultural representations mentioned above. I finally map out the gender strategies that are adopted by the women and men in the study and compare these strategies to their gender ideologies.

Finally, in chapter VI, I attempt a synthesis of the main arguments presented in the earlier chapters and show the different ways in which gender dynamics among the South Indian immigrants have been constructed and renegotiated. I review briefly some of the key debates between western and non-western feminists and make the claim that my study contributes to the emerging feminist discourse on 'Third World' diaspora. I also seek to demonstrate the relevance of my study to the scholarship on the Asian Indian diaspora. Further, I assert that an ethnography dealing with issues of gender, religion, and identity helps in understanding the rapidly changing cultural milieu of pluralistic society. I conclude by outlining some possibilities for further research in the sociology of gender and immigration in general and, more specifically, on the second generation Asian Indians in the US.

II

Understanding
Everyday Lives of Women

Feminist researchers have argued that traditional social theories have often marginalized or rendered insignificant women's participation. In the rare cases of women's experiences being included in conceptual schemes, they have been distorted. Mainstream social science research tended to incorporate 'gender' (or, more problematically, 'sex') as only one of the many sociological variables under study. Women scholars have for a long time been absorbed by the dominant rules of sociological method and have not been exceptional in their approaches to theory and research. Gradually, as feminist scholars started examining women's experiences more centrally, different strands of feminist theory have emerged.

Sandra Harding (1987; 1990) delineated three kinds of feminist epistemologies: feminist empiricism, feminist standpoint theory, and feminist postmodernism. Feminist empiricism identifies androcentrism and sexism as social 'biases' which need to be corrected by stricter adherence to the rules of scientific inquiry. It has been primarily used by researchers in biology and the social sciences. Harding points out that feminist empiricists work from the basic principle that 'both sexes have contributed to the evolution of our species'. So there is a call for inclusion of women as both the researched and the researcher. This kind of research has sought to generate 'good science' which, by definition, is not gender-blind. It involves 'adding women' to existing research agendas and giving recognition to them in their respective fields. Feminist empiricists challenge the incompleteness of scientific methods, but continue to employ the same methods in search of greater objectivity. They are critical of the dominant mode of scientific inquiry for neglecting gender and women's concerns and suggest that this 'bias' could be corrected by more rigorous empirical research.

Feminist standpoint theory attempts to work through the struggles of women to provide a less biased, less defensive, less perverse and, most of all, a more equal understanding of human relations. Standpoint feminists argue that the theoretical perspective offered by them and the methods they use to analyse society are from the perspective of the subjugated gender (Hartsock 1983; Smith 1974; Rose 1983). They are different from feminist empiricists because, for them, knowledge is grounded in experience.

A sociology for women preserves the presence of subjects as knowers and as actors. It does not transform subjects into the objects of study or make use of conceptual devices for eliminating the active presence of subjects. Its methods of thinking and its analytical procedures must preserve the presence of the active and experiencing subject (Smith 1987:105).

Dorothy Smith (1987) and other 'standpoint' feminists have adapted the Marxist vision in which science can reflect upon 'the way the world is' and work towards human emancipation. For the Marxists, it was through struggle in the workplace that the proletariat would generate knowledge. However, women never seemed to be part of this proletariat in any explicit manner. Women's emotional or reproductive labour were rendered invisible as were women's roles as social agents in the production of knowledge. Standpoint feminism sees women as the agents of knowledge. Women's experiences become resources for social analysis and it is women who should be able to reveal what women's experiences really are.

The subjugated gender cannot be seen as part of a binary opposition with the other gender, but it should be seen, as Smith insists, within the 'relations of ruling' of particular contexts. The concept of 'relations of ruling' focuses our attention on forms of knowledge; organized social institutions and practices; and questions of agency, consciousness and experience (Mohanty 1991). This concept deters analysts of gender from positing the universal standpoint of women as opposed to that of men and allows them to recognize that there are multiple standpoints located at the intersections of class, caste, race, gender, and religion. There are, therefore, standpoints of women that are particular to their specific contexts and experiences.[1]

Feminist postmodernism goes further than standpoint feminism in tackling questions of difference. Postmodernism challenges claims of universalism of any sort, including feminism. Postmodernists and feminists share a skepticism toward any universalizing claims regarding 'the existence, nature and powers of reason, progress, science, language and the "subject/self"' (Flax 1986:3). Multiple differences should be taken into account in theorizing without privileging any one (gender or race or class) over the other (Fraser and Nicholson 1990; Di Stefano 1990). But one of the problems that standpoint feminists and others have with postmodernism is that as we get caught up in postulating endless difference, gender loses its centrality. Some feminists have viewed this development, coming at a moment when feminist theory was just beginning to get accepted in mainstream academia, as potentially damaging to feminist politics (Hartsock 1987).

In my study, I do not privilege women's experiences over men's and neither do I argue about whose perspective is the more accurate one. I seek to understand women's particular experiences as we see them within their own contexts. As I mentioned in chapter I, I employ both the women-centred as well as gender-integrated approaches delineated by Lerner (1979). In parallel terms, my theoretical perspective borrows from both standpoint feminism and postmodern feminism. While claiming that women's experiences have not been adequately represented in the scholarship on immigrants, I am not suggesting that all immigrant women, irrespective of their race, class, and nationality, have homogeneous experiences. Specific studies on Jewish, Hispanic, Chinese, and Korean women might illuminate the similarities and differences between women in various diasporic communities. I have attempted to understand and interpret the experiences of Indian women in the United States from their own standpoints.

---

[1] Women share certain experiences as women because men in all cultures assign a certain otherness to them. Women, however, are differentiated along lines of race, class, religion, etc. and might find more similarities with men in their respective social contexts rather than with women of other groups. Recognizing this aspect of difference, standpoint feminists do not propagate some kind of feminine essentialism which assumes that all women share common experiences.

I have sought to give voice to the women in the Indian diaspora in Pittsburgh through intensive fieldwork. I was struggling in a new society, trying to be part of a diaspora while avoiding it at many times by assimilating completely into American graduate student life. It was my personal interest in the activities of the temple that led me to do fieldwork there. Often, feminist research begins from the researcher's own experience (Smith 1987). The purpose of this chapter is not only to inform the readers of the modalities of my research, but also to share with them some of my experiences as a sojourner in a particular part of the Indian diaspora. This sojourner role allowed me to observe the South Indian immigrants in Pittsburgh as a diasporic guest and enabled me to provide a 'view from below'.

Sociology and the methods of 'writing patriarchy' (especially positivist methods) have insisted on objectivity without really focusing on human experience. Although the phenomenologists and the ethnomethodologists have asked for a subjective account of everyday realities centering on experience, they too have ignored the experiences of women. I describe my work as a feminist ethnography because it focuses on the diaspora as a gendered reality, emphasizing standpoints of women. Feminist ethnography normally consists of three goals: to document the activities and lives of women; to understand and present women's experiences from their own viewpoints; to interpret women's behaviour as an expression of their particular social contexts (Reinharz 1992). Feminist fieldwork is similar to other kinds of fieldwork that entails the active involvement of the researcher in the production of social knowledge through direct participation in the activities she/he is attempting to comprehend. However, feminist fieldworkers find the necessity

of continuously and reflexively attending to the significance of gender as a basic feature of social life and . . . of understanding the social realities of women as actors. . . . [F]eminist fieldwork is aimed at giving voice to the experiences, perceptions, relationships, and realities of women through a reflexive, experiential form of analysis in which the researcher directly experiences these realities as a gendered-being and incorporates these experiences into her work (Dilorio 1982).

Thus, feminist theory and feminist movement inspire and guide the methods used by feminist scholars. Most feminist scholars advocate an inter-disciplinary approach to knowledge which grounds theory in women's everyday contexts (Stacey 1988).

My ethnography in the Pittsburgh temple focused on the significant roles assumed by women in the setting I chose. I have also interviewed women and men in the community to supplement and validate my participant observation data. Before I discuss the nature of my own ethnography I would like to describe in detail my field setting as well as the varied aspects of my data collection.

The Setting

The temple, a replica of the parent temple in Tirupati, is built in the South Indian style of architecture, according to the *Vaishnava* tradition. On the second floor of the building is the main worship area with the idols of Sri Venkateswara, Padmavathi, and Andal housed respectively in three main chambers. I did a considerable portion of my participant observation in the large hall (the *yagasala* or sacrifice room) outside the main sanctum sanctorum. The office, the reception area with the coat and shoe closets, the two auditoriums, the library with magazines and books from India, and the kitchen, are all located on the first floor. There is a parking lot at the lower level and land for further expansion of the temple.

The temple has four priests whose schedules are structured around the daily religious rituals. Regularly, there are different rituals from 9:00 a.m. to 8:00 p.m. Monday through Friday and some additional, special rituals on Saturday and Sunday when more worshippers and visitors are expected. The rituals that are performed on weekends are the more elaborate and expensive rituals. There are also optional rituals at particular times in the week for which individual devotees pay donations specified by the temple management. There are special *pujas* at the time of certain Hindu festivals that are performed according to the Hindu calendar. Sometimes the temple conducts massive, collective *pujas* which are organized on a grand scale involving elaborate ritual (with the *homam* or sacred fire). The Astalakshmi *puja* and Sudarsana *homam* (complex rituals for the prosperity of the family performed with the help of priests flown in from India), for instance, held in the summer of 1989, spanned over a period of ten days and were attended by about 7000 people from all over the country. Such events have become part of the temple's annual summer ritual calendar and other temples in North America look toward this pioneering institution in Pittsburgh for planning and institutionalizing such elaborate rituals.

Apart from religious activities, there is also the cultural aspect of the temple, the settings for which are the two auditoriums.[2] The smaller one can seat about a hundred people, while the larger one, inaugurated in 1991, can seat about four hundred and fifty people. Music, dance or drama programmes are held at the time of festivals and other social occasions. These cultural programmes often involve local children and adults, but highly-talented artists periodically visit from India to perform. The larger auditorium is built over a dining hall that is also used to perform weddings and to conduct other social events.

Every Sunday there are Sanskrit classes for adults and children and *Bharata Natyam* dance lessons for children (mostly girls), taking place simultaneously in different parts of the small auditorium which was often the setting for my participant observation. *Kuchipudi* dance classes began in 1991 on Saturday afternoons. Since the summer of 1992, language classes in Telugu and Tamil have been organized for interested children and adults. The language classes as well as the dance classes are taught by women. Music lessons are given every summer in other parts of the temple by male and female visitors from India. The temple organizes lectures by religious teachers many of whom come from the Vedantic Society in the US, while a few are also visiting religious teachers from India. At different times of the year religious classes are held for children, along with youth workshops, yoga classes, summer camps, and meditation sessions. The temple is involved in some charity activity, it provides scholarships to students graduating from high school, and organizes an annual graduation ceremony for outstanding Indian-American students. The kitchen provides a couple of South Indian rice-based items and snacks daily, and an additional breakfast item, *upma*, on weekends, at subsidized prices for the devotees. There are coke and juice machines in the corridor leading towards the kitchen.

The temple is managed essentially by a Board of Directors which is the highest decision-making body and the Executive

---

[2] The word 'religious' is being used here to refer to religious rituals while cultural includes music, arts and other traditions.

Committee which implements the decisions. The cultural, religious, publications, education, and youth and women's sub-committees are part of the executive committee. When I started my research in 1990, two other committees, the construction committee and the fund-raising committee, supervized the building of the larger auditorium. The members of these organizations are elected by the Trust Fund Committee and the corporate body, the latter being a much larger unit composed of over two hundred members who have been registered members for a period of time. Both the board and the various committees consist of a number of women who have assumed leadership roles in the temple. However, in the initial stages of the temple's establishment, there were more men than women in the *ad hoc* steering committee (Clothey 1983). Although the first treasurer of the temple was a woman, it is mainly in the past decade that a larger number of women have become active in the temple's administration.

Participant Observation

I did not live in the setting of my study as most researchers would in traditional ethnographic situations. Like the members of the group I observed, I lived in my own home and spent a great deal of time at the temple over a period of three years. No one except the priests and their families could live on the temple premises. As an ethnographer, therefore, I could not spend one hundred per cent of my time at the setting. Being a graduate student on a shoestring budget and struggling to earn a living by teaching did not help foster the kind of cultural immersion advocated by anthropologists. However, as Lynn Davidman (1991) found during her study of women returning to orthodox Judaism, having the space to type field notes, transcribe interviews, and reflect on the data away from the setting makes fieldwork much easier.

I began regular visits to the temple in mid-January of 1990 and continued data collection through the summer of 1992. Access was extremely easy; I had no problems gaining entry into the community. On each visit, I spent five to six hours in the different areas of the temple, making contacts and building rapport with potential interviewees. I initially set out to assess the amount and kind of participation of the various women and men who were regular visitors to the temple. I tried to attend almost every special religious ritual or cultural programme during this period, particularly on the weekends when the temple was at its busiest.

⸱ I visited the temple at different times of the day in order to get a holistic picture of the range of activities that took place. If I went on a Sunday morning, I would typically go to the main worship area, observe the weekly *abhishekam* (a ritual bath of the presiding deity's idol), and then stay and listen to a small group of people reciting a special prayer. I always entered the sanctum sanctorum and prayed along with other people, participating in the common rituals of worship. Then, I would either observe some of the other rituals like Satyanarayana *puja* or *kalyanam* (the wedding ceremony of the deities), or go downstairs to the auditorium to observe the dance class and the waiting mothers of the pupils. There were times when I would sit down either in the main worship area or the auditorium for the entire duration of the observation. On a festive occasion, I would generally move with the crowd by doing what they did: spending the duration of the ritual in the main worship area, then moving to the auditorium for the cultural programme, and finally joining in the traditional feast in the dining hall.

I always felt self-conscious about taking notes during these observations. I usually took notes when I was sitting alone, or came back home and typed up detailed notes. Sometimes, I would talk into the tape recorder while I was driving back home, so that I could provide a 'thick description' of events. On each occasion I ended up with several pages of participant observation notes to analyse. I would describe the surroundings, the numbers of people who were at the temple, the nature and type of interaction that took place between spouses, between strangers and among groups of people who spoke the same language. In my initial notes, I would describe every physical detail that I noticed, but later on my notes became more focused upon the interaction patterns between people and upon the analytic themes that emerged from the data.

I often faced an ethical dilemma about revealing my real purpose to the people at the temple, particularly on occasions when there was a large gathering. In a crowd situation it would have been ridiculous to go up and announce week after week that I was doing fieldwork. It was simpler to do it during more private conversations. Although the temple organization has a formal bureaucratic structure, the particular setting I described above did not require me to seek permission from any office-holder. Nonetheless, I mentioned to chairpersons of committees or directors of boards at different times that I was engaged in a project that focused on gender dynamics among immigrants who frequented the S.V. temple.

I was constantly moving between roles of an observer and a participant due to my specific insider/outsider status in the temple. I will discuss these issues at length later in this chapter.

Respondent Selection

My sample consisted of a total of forty people, fifteen men and twenty-five women. Many of the women were in professional or other jobs outside the home, some were students, a few homemakers. Most of them had at least a Bachelor's degree. All the men had at least a Master's or a professional degree and were employed in and around Pittsburgh. Eight out of my forty respondents had family incomes greater than $250,000; seventeen had family incomes between $100,000 and $200,000; twelve fell within the $50,000–100,000 range, while three were between $25,000–50,000. Those with lower incomes were people in their twenties and early thirties and in the initial stages of their careers. These income figures correspond with those of the Indian immigrant population as a whole in the United States cited earlier. Most of my respondents belonged to middle class and even lower-middle class families in India and have experienced upward mobility as immigrants. However, approximately a quarter of the people I interviewed had an upper-middle class status before immigration as well.

I selected as respondents only those people who were married and had at least one child, since children's future seemed, from initial conversations, to be one of the main motivations for parents' participation in the temple. Another condition for selection was that the respondents should have lived in Pittsburgh for at least two years. This was done so that the sample included only those who had had enough time to become a part of the South Indian community. I followed the purposive or theoretical sampling method, based on my own observations as well as on the recommendations of other informants. I wanted to include respondents who participated in a wide range of activities at the temple. I, therefore, chose my respondents based on the following characteristics, in addition to those mentioned above: involvement in the rituals at the main worship area; organization of and participation in cultural programmes; volunteering in the kitchen and/or at the office; participation in Sanskrit or other language classes; and elected membership in the board or committees.[3]

I discovered most of the respondents either through snowballing or through my own observations. Many of them were willing to provide names and introductions. The moment I spotted someone whom I thought would be a 'good respondent', based on the above criteria for respondent selection, I would try to get a closer look at the person to see if she or he was articulate or to see how I could get to know her/him better.

Interviewing

I conducted open-ended interviews on audio-tape which lasted about two hours on an average. Although I had a loosely structured interview guide, my interviews were free-wheeling conversations. The interview guide helped me focus my questions if we had wandered too far away from the intended line of discussion.

Some of the interviews were conducted in respondents' homes, some in the temple and a few in respondents' offices. If I went to people's homes, I often stayed on for lunch or dinner or accepted whatever food was offered to me. I was usually offered Indian food and sometimes had special food cooked in my honour. The temple became one of the locales for conducting interviews as many people spent a lot of time there and preferred to use that time for their interviews. Since a large percentage of their time on the weekend was spent at the temple, they felt they could spare a few hours during such days for my interview. Moreover, many of them were often waiting for a child to finish her/his class or for a spouse who was at a committee meeting. I usually interviewed a couple separately, except in the case of one couple who insisted on doing the interview together. I was concerned

---

[3] It is difficult to break them down by numbers because a lot of the people were active in two or more areas of the temple. For example, Urmila was the President of the Executive Committee and was also a keen participant in ritual activity.

that if I did joint interviews, the male voice of authority would subsume the woman's voice, not allowing the latter its free rein. However, in that particular case, it was the woman who completely dominated the interview and typically it was only when she went into the kitchen to check on dinner that her rather soft-spoken husband made his contribution.

Like Sarah Berk (1985) in her study of the 'gender factory' (i.e. the household), I also started interviewing men only to supplement the information I obtained from women, but unlike Berk I demanded the same kind of time and energy from the male respondents as I did from the women. Reinharz (1992) observes that feminist researchers disclose less and demand less when they interview people of higher social status and power, especially when they are men, but this was not the case with me. I volunteered an equal amount of information to the men as I did to the women. In fact some of my male respondents asked me more questions about my work and my family than did my female respondents. It was part of the respondents' curiosity about my own caste and class background that led to greater rapport between us. During one-on-one interviews, the men eased up considerably and some of my longest and most detailed interviews were with male respondents. However, after my data collection period, women continued to be friendly and show an interest in my work, but few of my male respondents engaged in more than a formal social greeting.

I was quite conscious of the fact that I had to adopt a 'view from below' rather than be the voice from above trying to 'objectify my subjects'. I was aware that 'the vertical relationship' that Maria Mies (1983) warns against must consciously be replaced by a relationship in which prominence and precedence should be given to the respondents' views rather than my own. Mies insists that the view from below has both a scientific as well as an ethical-political dimension. The data can be skewed even in so-called objective surveys because the respondent can be put off by the interrogative tone. I tried to make my respondents feel comfortable and most of the time my interviews were free-wheeling conversations where we shared a lot of information and they told me things of their own accord. I also recognized the fact that the relationship between the researcher and the researched should not be an exploitative one on either side.

Even though I adopted this view from below and there was a

clear difference in my social class and that of most of my respondents, I did not feel powerless in any situation.[4] After my respondents were assured of anonymity and confidentiality, they offered detailed accounts of not only the temple, but also of different aspects of their lives as immigrants. I did not have a problem in persuading most of them to talk as I told them that the more they shared their experiences with me, the richer my data would be. Following an interview with someone, I would observe that person's behaviour in the temple more closely, in order to make connections between their actions and what they had said in their interviews. On occasion I got a little disturbed when something I saw directly contradicted something a respondent had told me about herself. I tried to extract some sense out of these contradictions between word and action by going back to the respondent to clarify the confusion. I never had a problem walking up to a complete stranger and asking them to become a respondent. I also showed some of them my work and sought their opinions on the issues I wrote about.

Making Sense of the Data

Following Anselm Strauss, my data collection, observation, coding and categorizing of the data were conducted simultaneously (as far as possible) so that several levels of analysis could constantly feed back into one another (Strauss 1987; Glaser and Strauss 1967). However, on several occasions during fieldwork, it was impossible to keep up, on the one hand with typing up the notes from my observations and transcribing interviews and, on the other, with analysing that data the same day. I went through a few sessions of observation and some interviews without doing any analysis for days and then would come back to my computer and catch up on the analysis. The analysis continued long after data collection.

Initially, I quickly read over the transcript of each interview and set of field notes and jotted down a largely impressionistic cluster of categories on the margins of the transcripts. I then proceeded to do, what Strauss calls, 'open coding'. This was unrestricted coding of the interview, paragraph by paragraph enabling me to fracture

---

[4] However, my class of origin (educated, professional, urban, upper-middle) in India was equal to or higher than many of my respondents' original class.

the data analytically and leading me towards a higher degree of conceptualization. Descriptive and analytic categories were created in the process of this coding. Although this initial process was relatively unrefined, it allowed me not only to raise important questions to be pursued in further interviews and keep my eyes open for things that I might have missed before, but also to begin some interpretation, however tentative, of gender dynamics among the immigrants at the temple. While the coding scheme was being developed, detailed 'analytic memos' were written. For example, I have several analytic memos on the theme of cultural reproduction and the socialization of children. The next phase of analysis involved what Strauss calls 'axial coding', which is a more rigorous analysis done around one dimension or core category at a time. At this stage, I subdivided a broader category such as cultural reproduction into axes or sub-themes like gendered socialization, effects of acculturation on cultural reproduction, etc. As the analysis progressed, I wrote more analytic memos, refining some of the older ones and creating new ones, parts of which have ended up in various places in this document.

My analysis was influenced by the feminist theory that I had read and was quite familiar with. I recognized the gendered nature of cultural reproduction and realized that a conventional study of the temple would be done by making women a part of the temple structure, not as conscious agents of change in the Indian diaspora, particularly in the religious sphere. It was the experiences of the women that took a predominant place in my analysis. I accept that my own beliefs and interests largely influenced the interpretation of the reality experienced in the Indian diaspora. I believe, with Sandra Harding (1987) and other feminist scholars, that the introduction of the subjective element into the analysis increases the objectivity of the research and that self-reflexivity actually validates the data. This is one of the principles that is crucial for the study of women. Any attempt to erase the marks of the researcher's presence would be contradictory to the idea of a feminist ethnography. Further, objectivity would have been enhanced if the respondents had directly participated in the study by taking an active role in analysing and making sense of the data (Acker et al. 1983). This did not take place to the extent that I would have liked as my respondents were content to talk to me, but not very curious about what I actually did with the data.

THE NATURE OF EXPERIENTIAL RESEARCH

My interaction with my respondents must be seen in the context of my own status as an upper-caste, middle class, female doctoral student in the same city. Nowhere in the study do I claim to be the invisible researcher whose anonymous voice of authority looms large over the subjects of study. My own beliefs about women and men and the Hindu religion changed to some extent during the research process. The experiential data I collected led me to different levels of understanding of the people I met, observed, and interviewed. My notes sometimes reflected my own recently-evoked interest in those dynamics that I might have previously ignored. For instance, I would develop an interest in a particular religious ritual mainly because some of my female respondents were rather involved in it. I became a much better listener, often returning to a particular respondent to ask a question that had been nagging me since our last meeting.

Many of the people I interviewed, especially women, felt empowered in the process of sharing information about their lives. They told me that it was good that I was writing about their lives and about their activities at the temple because people who read my account might be inspired to build a similar temple in their own cities. There are also some who felt that their lives were not important enough to record and often asked, 'why me?' Interestingly enough, most of the people who asked this question were women. It is in this context that I feel that listening to these women's voices and giving them an empathetic space in scholarly work is important. As Dorothy Smith writes:

The standpoint of women . . . is a method that, at the outset of inquiry, creates the space for an absent subject, and an absent experience that is to be filled with the presence and spoken experience of actual women speaking of and in the actualities of their everyday lives (Smith 1987:107).

My work among economically privileged upper class and upper-middle class Indian women in a wealthy nation surely does not have any emancipatory goals and it is not research *for* women in any viable sense.[5] Research that highlights women's problems such

---

[5] Research *for* women is distinguished from research *on* or *about* women in that it incorporates a theory of change and an emancipatory objective in research (Klein 1983; Mies 1978). But if feminists continue to distinguish the women's movement that involves fighting for equal rights on the street (public

as domestic violence among the diasporic Indians is useful, but it is dangerous to universalize the problems faced by Indian women in the West and present pictures of a victimized Indian woman in the diaspora. There are certain strands of feminist research that focus almost exclusively on the study of women who are the victims of male dominance. Studies of rape, domestic violence, pornography and other crimes against women have brought about greater public consciousness of some of the serious problems women face. These studies which examine the violent forms of patriarchy, however, tend to portray women only as victims. These victimologies underplay women's agency; their active role in resisting patriarchy and as agents of social change are neglected.

I think it is critical that I write about the lives of the immigrant Indian women whose voices have hitherto remained unheard. I am not claiming here that these women have been passive victims until now and that my work aids them in finding a voice. On the contrary, I assert that the South Indian immigrant women in my study have transformed gender relations in the community through their everyday lives, although few are fully conscious of that achievement. None of these women are self-proclaimed feminists and they did not think that I would gain much by speaking with them. By writing about the active role of women in the creation of the Indian diaspora, I hope not only to create an awareness about their lives but also do so from their own standpoints. I wanted to uncover the power experienced by these women in what is traditionally, a patriarchal institution. A feminist orientation helps in confronting certain androcentric biases and allows the participant observer to see women not as passive followers of their husbands and fathers but as fully active members of their social, cultural, and economic worlds.

It was indeed difficult to bracket my own feminist beliefs and sociological perspectives and see things from the points of view of the women in my study. I did not think that it would serve my

---

space) and the emancipation of women as experienced by women at home and in the workplace, we fall into the androcentric distinction of making separate gendered spheres. I assert that whatever their class or caste background, women's experiences cannot be ignored or, worse still, subsumed under pressures of androcentric paradigms and analyses.

function as an ethnographer well if I tried to establish ideological compatibility with my respondents. Reinharz (1992:67) says that if both the researcher and the researched are feminist, it raises questions that are quite different from situations where one is feminist and the other is not. It was apparent that I differed ideologically with many of my respondents, but I did not seek to engage them in feminist debates which would have, in the given situation, made me appear patronizing towards them. Even without such ideological compatibility, I thought I could make a sincere effort to understand the women for who they are and what they are doing. Feminist ethnographer, Susan Stall believes that feminists are better able to see changes in other women's lives when they do not impose their own values and judgements upon them. According to her,

If we utilize liberal . . . feminist arguments that emphasize abstract and universal conceptions of equality as the basis for meaningful political activity for women, we may be oversimplifying our understanding of the roots of social resistance and innovation in the everyday experience of women. . . . Current feminist arguments about political action are limiting and inadequate because they do not take into account the complexity of women's lived experience within community, and thus reinforce and call for political activities which are similarly limiting (Stall 1985).

As a participant observer, I empathized only to some extent with the feelings of the people I was studying. Most of the immigrants, both male and female, thought about their children's future and their own identities. For someone like me who is not a mother and is younger than most of the people I was studying, it was not easy to understand the degree of motivation and the intensity of their desire to help provide their children with an 'Indian' identity. In the words of anthropologist James Clifford (1988:25), fieldworkers' inability to 'inhabit indigenous minds, . . . is a permanent, unresolved problem of ethnographic method'.

However, as time went by, it became easier to see things from their perspective. Interacting with people from different class and ethnic backgrounds and observing their activities at the temple helped me make sense of many things that were earlier beyond the limits of my comprehension. I learnt that as a feminist researcher one is often quite susceptible to falling into a judgmental trap and evaluating the actions of other women as passive conformity or subservience to patriarchal values and norms.[6] But, as my experience with the Indian immigrant women in Pittsburgh taught me, empowerment can be felt in more ways than one. These feelings of empowerment surfaced particularly when these women compared themselves with their mothers and with other women back home. I adopted the comparative approach in many of my questions and this helped them to reflect aloud on their lives in a broader context.

The Observer Observed

The attitudes of my respondents toward my project ranged from genuine interest and appreciation to indifference and even amazement. Those who felt that the work I was doing would benefit the community were extremely interested and felt that my work would help them understand the needs of Hindu immigrants. Some of them suggested that I speak with their children and get their perspectives on some of the issues bothering the community. I got the distinct feeling that some of these parents thought that I could serve as a mediator between the two generations. Perhaps some of them thought that I might be able to debunk some of the popular myths about Indian culture that their children had internalized from mass media or tell them about some of the realities about life 'back home' that they had no other ways of knowing.

Some of my respondents expressed an interest in reading my work after it is completed. One respondent, Ratna, who was the chairperson of the board of directors a few years ago, suggested that I approach the board for possible funding of my research. I did not pursue this as I thought it would not be ethical for me to seek funding from the very institution I was studying. But the suggestion, coming as it did from one of the leaders in the temple organization, made me feel that my work was recognized as important to the new immigrant community. There were others who

---

[6] When standards of evaluation of an 'objective' observer do not match those of the observed, judgements tend to be skewed and, as in the case of the 'First World' observing the 'Third World' particularly, reproduces ethnocentrism and results in the imposition of cultural categories. Although this is not the case with my study, I myself have been trained according to the western system of education and might fall into a similar trap.

were eager to help me by introducing me to prospective respondents, particularly to those they felt were key people in the community. Whenever I encountered willing respondents it helped me come to terms with any reservations I had about the exploitation of 'research subjects' by me as an ethnographer (Stacey 1988).

Not everyone, however, shared unbridled enthusiasm for my work. Some wondered why I was even bothering them and tried to put me off. I was persistent because I felt that they were going to be 'key informants', and would eventually get most interviews but I had to let go in a couple of cases. Among those who were initially reluctant were two men and a woman who were concerned about the trust factor. After I spoke with them at length about my study, they seemed quite satisfied and opened up to me without further problems. One of the men, Arun, had an earlier experience with another researcher who had not revealed his complete agenda to the people involved.[7] Some of my respondents asked me why I needed to do a study about them and were surprised to know that I came all the way from India to do sociology unlike most other compatriots pursuing studies in engineering or computer science. For the most part, the Indian diaspora considers few professions, besides medicine, engineering, and computer science, as respectable and worthy of their attention. Social sciences and humanities are certainly not among the privileged realms of study and if one is in those disciplines it could not be out of choice; it could mean you were not bright enough to get into the more lucrative fields. This attitude reflects the upper-middle class, professional status of many Indians. I distinctly remember the reaction I got from a female physician: 'I can't imagine why you would be interested in doing something like this for a Ph.D. dissertation.' I had interviewed her earlier and told her that the topic excited me enough to pursue it further for a doctoral degree. For a while I was quite upset and just brooded over my work without going to the field for a few days. Of course it did not take me too long

---

[7] It is possible that some of the information I obtained from respondents who were initially hesitant about being interviewed is different from that gathered in interviews with more willing respondents. For example, Arun was particularly critical of what he considered to be the parochial attitudes of many in the South Indian community, a feeling not expressed by other, more willing respondents. In fact, it is possible that his initial reluctance was related to this opinion which he might not have wanted to share with/an 'outsider'.

to realize that some people had a difficult time understanding not only that somebody could actually make a career out of such commonplace social curiosities, but also seek to do so by using the 'soft and fluffy' techniques of qualitative research rather than the more acceptable statistical methods. I decided it was not my primary goal to convert them either to the merits of social science or to the benefits of qualitative methods.

Some people misunderstood my interest in certain aspects of the temple and in their own religious practices. They assumed that the nature of my interest in every aspect of the rituals was as personal as theirs. For instance, Malathi and her husband, who were involved in establishing a different temple of their own, wondered why I did not display a sustained interest in their venture. I had originally interviewed her since she was constantly at the temple. She seemed like the perfect candidate for my study as she lived only a mile away from the temple and visited it once or twice a day. It was only after my interview with her that I discovered that she was looking for prospective donors and devotees for her new temple and obviously misread my overtures. This temple was particularly for believers of Shirdi Sai Baba, an Indian saint, and I was not really interested in studying the formation of this group in Pittsburgh. As I repeatedly turned down invitations to participate in their activities, Malathi seemed disappointed that the new temple had lost one of its prospective worshippers. For a long time I used to continue to speak with people like Malathi and try to understand their relationships with the temple, not knowing that many had their own agendas and that I might become a part of that agenda.

Being a student in a transitional status automatically places one on a lower rung in the ladder of social stratification than those who are permanent residents or citizens of the US. The large number of Indian students at the University of Pittsburgh, Carnegie Mellon, and Duquesne University have never really been considered an integral part of the local Indian community in Pittsburgh. In our transitory student status, few of us were likely to be in Pittsburgh after we graduated. The Indians who frequented the temple saw themselves as deeply entrenched in the temple's structure, while the rest of us were a floating population who were treated like visitors or sojourners rather than as full-fledged members of the community. But by spending time as a researcher at the temple, I did not feel like a mere visitor as I had gained adequate legitimacy among the people I was studying and was an insider on many levels.

INSIDER/OUTSIDER ISSUES

Recent work on the need for reflexivity in ethnographic research emphasizes that a faithful representation of reality must be both similar to that reality and distinct from it (Woolgar 1988). This issue of representation can also be problematized in relation to the degree of affinity between the researcher and the researched. The researcher's own identity and how it is perceived by the researched significantly influence the ethnography as well as the analysis emerging out of it. It is, therefore, important to lay bare the researcher's own position *vis-à-vis* the respondents. According to Harding,

The best feminist analysis . . . insists that the inquirer her/himself be placed in the same critical plane as the overt subject matter, thereby recovering the entire research process for scrutiny in the results of research . . . the class, race, culture, and gender assumptions, beliefs and behaviours of the researcher her/himself must be placed within the frame of the picture that s/he attempts to paint (Harding 1987:9).

Perhaps the most significant aspect of my ethnographic work in this setting was that I myself was a South Indian Hindu expatriate woman. There are different levels at which this particular identity operated for me as a researcher. There is a great advantage in being an 'insider' who could blend fully into the specific cultural environment. I belonged to the same religion, had similar ethnic origins, and spoke the same language as many of the people who frequented the temple. The Indian clothes I normally wore to the temple and to people's homes facilitated this immersion in the community. My dress and language use helped me gain easy access to the setting and to establish contacts with potential respondents. I repeatedly demonstrated respect for tradition by being at the temple for almost every important religious and cultural occasion, many times participating actively in the performance of rituals.

The fact that I was an 'insider' to the community was established by the degree of informality people displayed around me, taking my presence for granted. Sometimes people did not fully comprehend the reasons for my spending so much time at the temple.

This curiosity was particularly evident when they spotted me hanging around dance classes where children practised for upcoming performances under the watchful eyes of their mothers. On many occasions some of the women tried in vain to recruit me for group dances or dramas staged for festivals. When I would excuse myself by saying either that I was too busy with my studies or that I did not have the talent, they wondered how I would have so much time to hang around at the temple and yet refuse to be a part of such activities. My reluctance to participate in activities like dance, did not deter them from treating me as an insider, with those who knew about my study taking me for granted and others perceiving me as one of the many curious onlookers.

I became so much a part of their discussions and gossip about people that I gradually began to assume the role of a daughter of the community. The women exhibited greater warmth and informality than did the men, who seemed less willing to give details about their lives in group situations. Many women, for instance, sympathized with me for being away from my family and affectionately volunteered tips about where to buy the cheapest Indian groceries or shared a recipe for a favourite dish. In an ethnography about the life of a Kung woman, Marjorie Shostak (1983) wrote: 'With older women I went further, presenting myself as a child in need of help in preparing for what life might yet have to offer.' I often saw my mother, who lived 10,000 miles away, in many of these women and sought emotional comfort in getting their advice about little things. I accepted invitations to parties at their homes and gained deeper access to the diasporic community. This not only allowed me to get to know people much better, but also made me feel that I was able to pursue my research goals even outside the confines of the temple, which I had assigned to myself as an ethnographic site. I felt guilty that most of the time I was analysing the actions of my hostesses rather than treating it as a mere social event that required a great deal of participation.

However, I did not want the role of the 'daughter of the community' to hamper the fragile identity of an adult researcher that I was struggling to sustain for myself. I preferred to avoid total immersion at all times, except when I was taking part in a particular religious ritual for my own fulfilment. Some feminist researchers like Diane Bell (1983) and Karen McCarthy Brown (1985) believe that such immersion is, in fact, the best way to obtain information and learn more about the people in their studies. Although I was far from being a complete outsider, I felt the need to maintain a certain amount of detachment from the people in my study. Therefore, I did not develop any close and long-lasting friendships of the kind Ann Oakley (1985) encourages feminist researchers to develop during their work.

Whenever I solicited information about the administration of the temple, I was clearly an outsider. It was impossible for me to observe the formal board meetings at the temple as a full participant, as only elected members and committee volunteers could attend these meetings. When I did volunteer to do any work at the temple, it was only on an informal basis rather than as a registered volunteer.[8] If the focus of my study had been organizational dynamics of this institution, perhaps it would have been useful to become an insider or a member of the temple's committees, as did sociologist Patricia Baker (1987), who became a bank-teller during her fieldwork in a Canadian bank.

One of my respondents, Urmila, told me that I had a lot to offer the community as I was an 'outsider' with relatively weaker emotional ties to the temple. She thought it would be good for them to get a perspective from the 'outside'. I was an outsider to her because I was in Pittsburgh as a student and not as an immigrant. By categorizing me as an outsider, this respondent provided the kind of distance I was seeking during my fieldwork. However, in feminist sociologist Susan Krieger's (1985) words, 'we are not, in fact, ever capable of achieving the analytic "distance" we have long been schooled to seek.'

I became conscious that not being a mother was another major factor in my getting categorized as an outsider. Most of the students or spouses of students I knew who were active in the temple were those who had children of their own, a factor which made it much easier for them to earn the insider status. Parenthood, especially motherhood, enhances one's acceptance in the community, and rituals such as baby showers welcome the expectant mother into the community of mothers. The fact that the field I chose was not an exclusively female one, but a mixed gender setting helped me maintain a certain degree of detachment. Although the

---

[8] The temple has various committees that need volunteers to periodically participate in some of the activities. They maintain lists of volunteers and allot them duties whenever they are needed.

men at the temple were quite friendly, they were more formal respondents than the women. The social interaction is quite gendered in the temple and my identity as a researcher and an outsider was more obvious in male areas than it was in female settings. Men tended to be more formal, and even those who conversed in Telugu informally would speak in English (particularly during interviews) when they knew about my project. This could be due to the fact that English has been the medium for formal or official communication in post-colonial India. The Indian middle class was often socialized into speaking in English on formal occasions. It was more common for the women rather than the men to speak to me in Telugu which usually generated a more informal situation.

Linguistic and Regional Boundaries

Another dimension of the insider/outsider issue was the divisions within the diaspora on the basis of language, region, caste, and other ethnic boundaries. As a southerner from India, I was an insider in a South Indian temple. However, the label 'South India' usually encompasses four different states where people speak four different languages. I am from the state of Andhra Pradesh and I speak Telugu, so I was automatically claimed by the Telugus in Pittsburgh as an insider, while I became an outsider to the people from other regional and linguistic groups.

It was fascinating to see the number of ways in which ethnic boundaries operated during my research. One of the first questions many people asked me was what language I spoke. When I told them I spoke Telugu, they would instantly break into Telugu if they themselves spoke the language. One of my respondents, Rajni, who was very active in the temple, told me that she kept the addresses and phone numbers of Indian immigrants sorted according to the language spoken. Most other people, similarly, made friends with those who spoke the same language. This was true especially for people who were originally from semi-urban or rural India, regions which had more or less linguistically homogeneous populations. People usually recommended as respondents others from the same region or those who spoke the same language. I could not speak to non-Telugus unless they spoke English and I had two interviews in Telugu with women who did not speak

English. Thus, the linguistic and regional divisions in the temple influenced my data collection to some extend. But apart from the problem of the actual mechanics of data collection, I felt that there was a constant need to be and feel a Telugu. There were occasions when there was the celebration of 'Teluguness' in the form of a cultural event and there were particular kinds of food items that represented ethnic origins. I was constantly asked to participate in such occasions.

Locals vs Visitors to Pittsburgh

The insider/outsider division takes on yet another form in the boundary between local Pittsburghers, and out-of-town visitors. It is not uncommon to find in the temple parking lot, cars from Ontario, Michigan, and Florida besides those from states closer to Pennsylvania. During long weekends like Memorial Day, the Fourth of July, and Labour Day, the temple organizes special ceremonies as devotees from all over the east coast and the mid-west are expected. On these occasions, the Pittsburghers play host and volunteer to organize these massive events.

By the time I concluded my fieldwork, I knew, at least by face, most of the locals who frequented the temple. It was not difficult, therefore, to pick out the outsiders from the way they dressed, from their curious walks through the temple, and from their general demeanour. For most of them, it is a pilgrimage and an extremely nostalgic experience, perhaps the next best thing to visiting a temple in India. Many of the women would be dressed in silks and wore a lot of jewellery. The men too would sometimes dress in traditional dhoti-kurta and would usually be seen together with the rest of the family. A local Pittsburgher would be dressed in simpler clothes unless it was a festival or some other big function and families rarely stuck together.

Despite the fact that my study was about the people who live around the Greater Pittsburgh area, I often spoke with people who came to the temple from outside, which helped me look at the Pittsburghers from a different point of view. Most of them said they felt very close to the deity and enjoyed their visit to the temple. Some of the outsiders would look on enviously as the children in Pittsburgh learned music and dance, bemoaning the lack of such cultural opportunities for their own children.

In spite of my own ambivalence as an insider/outsider, I some-times suggested ideas about temple activities and shared some of my own experiences as a researcher with my respondents. I refused, however, to be dragged into arguments about other people or about the different ways of coping with acculturation and assimilation, since that would have conflicted with my basic purpose. Being an insider might have resulted in my taking certain things for granted, things that would have looked different through the eyes of a non-Hindu. One of my respondents, Rajni, talked about a film made by an American about the temple that captured subtle details which an insider would have missed. In sum, while I concede that I might have lost subtle insights that could have been gained by a complete outsider, I believe that my uniquely ambivalent location as both an insider and an outsider to the community led me into paths that might have been inaccessible to a total stranger. It was, to paraphrase Alfred Schutz, a case of trying to make the familiar strange and the strange familiar.

Exit

An interesting outcome of the insider/outsider dilemmas I had experienced was the difficulty of actually exiting the field. Even after I had formally concluded my fieldwork at the temple, my lingering researcher instincts did not make it easy for me to just go and participate in a *puja* or enjoy a dance performance like everybody else. My eyes used to keep wandering, observing people, particularly those I interviewed, making mental notes about their interaction with others, and cross-checking information offered to me during interviews. Sometimes I would feel guilty that I no longer seemed to be able to look at people without seeing them as participants in my study or as providers of data. I continued to go to parties in the community and felt that my female respondents probably began to accept me as one of them. However, men continued to be formal with me and made enquiries about my work.

I did not feel that I had to cut myself off from the temple and make a clean exit in the conventional ethnographic sense. Most researchers are ready to leave when they feel that their 'welcome was wearing out' (Warner 1988:85). But I was too much of an insider to feel unwelcome. I miss not only the city which was my home for five years, but also the temple to which I have grown quite attached. I would like to know how these children, whose parents are so concerned about their future, turn out when they grow up. I would also like to get in touch with a few of my respondents and show them my final work. I really exited my field only when I left the United States to come back home to India. Now I am no longer part of the diaspora, but continue to identify with the people in Pittsburgh and hope to go back there at some point to show them my work.

In many ways my entry into the field was not a formal event and neither was my exit. My ethnography will, therefore, remain, in the words of Clifford and Marcus (1986:7), *'partial* — committed and incomplete.'

III

Cultural Reproduction and the Reconstruction of Identities

A rjun Appadurai characterizes the immigrant predicament as one in which they face 'the seductiveness of plural belonging, of becoming American while staying somehow diasporic, of an expansive attachment to an unbounded fantasy' (Appadurai 1993: 422). In this chapter I will examine some aspects of this diasporic condition, as represented by the cultural practices of Indian immigrants in the United States, focusing especially on how gender relations are perpetuated and reconstructed through these practices.

Immigrants carry with them, from their countries of origin, culturally imagined roles and values which complicate the process of acculturation (Fong and Peskin 1973).[1] Many immigrants prefer to retain their ethnic distinctiveness in a plural society rather than assimilate into a non-existing melting pot (Hirschman 1983). One of the ways immigrant groups cope with the alien environment is by remaining allied to the values and ideologies of their cultures of origin. Another coping strategy is to try to integrate aspects of both the parent and host cultures that are felt to be most amenable to the development of self-esteem and identity (Sue 1973). Whatever strategy they might adopt, immigrants are primarily concerned with 'cultural reproduction' or the process by which they seek to transmit their knowledge, values, belief systems, and behavioural norms to the next generation (Mallea 1988). This idea

[1] Acculturation has usually been defined as culture change that results from continuous first-hand contact between two distinct cultural groups (Redfield et al. 1936).

of reproduction cannot be conceptualized merely as a mechanistic replication, but as a generative process involving innovation and creativity (Jenks 1993:5). Possibilities of change and new combinations in cultural reproduction become particularly significant in the immigrant context.

Raymond Williams has written that emigration involves a 'crisis of epistemology' that focuses people's attention on their traditions or narrative in order to establish a 'known world' (Williams 1988:31). One way in which Hindu immigrant groups try to resolve this crisis is by building temples and establishing indigenous social and cultural activities in the new society. The salience of religion for early immigrants to the United States was noted in several studies including Herberg's classic work, *Protestant-Catholic-Jew* (Herberg 1955) and in Miller and Marzik (1977). Herberg describes the transformation of America from the land of immigrants to the 'triple melting pot' comprising of three major religious faiths, Protestantism, Catholicism and Judaism. While the second generation immigrants tried to assimilate into the American culture, the third generation sought to discover their origins. He says that it was the 'dialectic of the third generation interest' in their heritage that made religion an important form of identity in the United States.

. . . what he (the grandson) can 'remember' is obviously not his grandfather's foreign language, or even his culture; it is rather his grandfather's *religion* — America does not demand of him the abandonment of the ancestral religion as it does of the ancestral language and culture (Herberg 1955:257).

Religion is an accepted part of the 'American way of life' and by the middle of the twentieth century religion was firmly institutionalized. Herberg goes further to explain that America has emerged as a three-religion nation and anyone who was anything but a Protestant, Catholic or Jew was a 'foreigner'. Four decades after Herberg's classic work, the three religions continue to be the dominant ones in the United States, but the arrival of people of many other religions and the consequent move toward cultural pluralism has made the slow acceptance of other religions possible. In the case of Indian immigrants, it is still the first generation which forms the diaspora in the United States and they have made a visible attempt to institutionalize religion. A number of recent studies have shown that Indian immigrants have retained their religious values and other forms of cultural expression regardless of the country to which they have emigrated (Clothey 1983; Saran 1985; Burghart 1987; Williams 1988; Segal 1991).

Immigrant religious institutions are not only places of worship but centres for various cultural and social activities that bind the participants into a close-knit community. In Pittsburgh, the S.V. temple was conceived by its members to be

more than a religious institution! It is a cultural centre — a place of dialogue — for Indian adults to reaffirm their heritage — for their children to discover who they are — for all Americans as a reminder of the diversity that has shaped this country (*Saptagiri Vani*, 1979:3).

South Indian immigrant women who frequent the temple play a crucial role in this process of reaffirming their cultural heritage and in shaping the identities of their children. As part of an elite group of people who emigrated from India in the pursuit of professional success, the South Indian immigrants have the resources to engage in representations of the past and reconstruct identities for themselves and their children. The identities that are built and the memories that are invoked in the process are not fixed in space and time, but are constructions of reality that change over time (Gillis 1994). The South Indian immigrant women play a central role in creating a familiar world for themselves as well as for their families.

Nostalgia and the Celebration of Community

An important feature of deterritorialized groups such as immigrants is that they dwell in 'imagined worlds' (Appadurai 1990). Nostalgia is the critical building material for the construction of such an imagined world, a new cultural space, inhabited by the diasporic individuals. The word 'diaspora' implies the dispersal of people and their eventual return to the homeland and this idea is often sustained by nostalgia. An *archetypal diaspora* comprises of a group whose members seek to hold on to an 'imaginal memory' that includes the idea of return (Armstrong 1982). In the case of the Indian diaspora the idea of return is not necessarily a physical, but a cultural phenomenon (Nadarajah 1994). The building of the temple in Pittsburgh can be seen as an expression of nostalgia, symbolizing an act of cultural return. By reproducing the 'authentic' architectural style (that of its parent temple in Tirupati), the community demonstrated its resolve to recreate and reproduce a familiar cultural institution in an alien world. Clothey sees the temple as affirming 'a world — a psychic space — in which the community lives and acts out its identity' (Clothey 1983:196). Temples have been a central part of South Indian culture in India, and this centrality is also visible in the building of temples by South Indian Hindus in the various countries to which they have moved.

Many respondents reported that their first visit to the temple made them feel like they were in India. Some compared it to the temple in Tirupati, while others said they were 'thrilled' to see a temple such as this one in a foreign land. One woman noted that the temple was 'really authentic' and on each visit she made a special effort to dress traditionally as she felt she was 'going to India'. Perceptions of the temple's 'authenticity' are clearly based on nostalgic images of the temple in Tirupati which they had visited several years ago. Another expression of nostalgia can be seen in the yearning among many women to celebrate festivals as their mothers would have done back home. They try their best to replicate the ceremonies as closely as possible.

Although it was obvious from my research that men share this nostalgia, it is the women, in their traditional roles as transmitters of culture, who take a more active part in giving these memories a concrete shape in the form of festivals, ethnic food, dress, and religious and language classes. 'Memory work', like any other kind of labour, is carried out within a complex set of gender, class, and power relations which determine who 'remembers' what and to what purpose (Gillis 1994). Gillis argues that women, more often than men, tend to serve as unpaid keepers and embodiments of memory. While the men are on the 'fast track' of individualism in American society, it is the women who are expected to stay in touch with the past and remind the men of their cultural background. One of my male respondents, Rajaraman lamented that his wife was not creative enough to celebrate festivals at home. If she had some interest, he would have 'helped' her with the festivities but, he said, he 'could not' initiate something that was traditionally the responsibility of the women. So, there is the expectation that women have to not only remember the past but also to reproduce it.

Nostalgic feelings may also be directed toward some non-religious aspects of their past such as language, culture, or their hometowns. However, for many there is also what Jameson (1989) called a 'nostalgia for the present'. The paradox here is that immigrants experience a nostalgia for not only what they left behind in the past but also for what is inaccessible to them in the present. Regular visits to the home country as well as exposure to contemporary cultural products (such as the latest movies on video and fashion trends) enable immigrants to refresh their memories and to keep up with the changing cultural milieu back home. Robertson (1992:159) argues that late twentieth century nostalgia is quite 'consumerist'. The Indian immigrants' desire for such things as the latest ethnic fashions, jewellery, spices, and specialty foods, which they can easily acquire through global capitalism, is an example of a nostalgia that is indeed embedded in a consumerist culture.

All these expressions of nostalgia among the Indian immigrants reinforce a deeply held belief that the entire group or subgroups within it have a common ancestry, a common history, a common present, and a common immigrant situation.[2] It is this belief that the many ethnic group events in the temple ritualize. Often the longing to maintain symbolic and emotional links with the past is the driving force for being a regular visitor to the temple. Thus, the Indian immigrant group is not merely a moral community in the sense of a religious group, but in Robert Bellah's phrase, 'a community of memory.'

In order not to forget that past, a community is involved in retelling its story, its constitutive narrative, and in so doing, it offers examples of the men and women who have embodied and exemplified the meaning of the community. These stories of collective history and exemplary individuals are an important part of the tradition that is so central to a community of memory (Bellah et al. 1985:153).

The immigrants who frequent the temple see themselves as part of a *Gemeinschaft*, participating collectively not only in worship but also in a celebration of their nostalgia and community spirit. For instance, a festival gathering certainly serves more than a religious function.

[2] At least they aspire to make their history seem uniform and on festive occasions attempt to underplay the differences that are present.

The Social Functions of Religion

During some festivals, scenes from famous Hindu myths and epics are often performed in the temple auditorium. The atmosphere is that of a wedding or any other big social event in India. Many of the women and men I interviewed made statements like 'I think the temple is a *social* [emphasis mine] place where we can meet a lot of friends'. They said they derive a sense of belonging through participation in group activities. Forty-one year old Suneeta would come to the temple from Johnstown, about sixty miles from Pittsburgh, at least a couple of times a week so that she could meet and talk to people in Kannada (her native language), something that she says she could not do in Johnstown. In the words of forty-four year old Urmila who is very active in the temple's administration:

The temple is more of a social centre and I do like to meet people. We sit in the temple and exchange whatever has been happening in our lives. In fact I sometimes spend only five minutes upstairs [in the main worship area], when I do *namaskaram* in a hurry to all the gods, and then spend the rest of the time talking with friends and attending meetings.

Urmila is quite conscious that the religious aspect of the temple visit is almost secondary to the social one. The idea of religion performing a social function is quite Durkheimian. For Durkheim, religion was a mode of representing social realities. He saw religion as performing social functions, both as a system of communication of ideas and sentiments and as a means of specifying and regulating social relationships. For him, 'social life, in all its aspects and in every period of its history, is made possible only by a vast symbolism' (Durkheim 1915:264).

The need for the temple is felt very strongly, particularly, at a time when the second generation is in the process of 'becoming American'. Many parents expressed the sentiment that going to the temple establishes for their children some roots within the traditional culture. Fifty year old Ratna, a woman who has two teenage sons remarked:

I try to bring them to the religious and cultural activities, not only for the religious experience, but for the social one. . . . On *Ugadi* (the Telugu and Kannada New Year), for instance, I would like them to be a part of the event and also mingle with friends. I think that it should be a part of their growing up. They should feel comfortable coming to the temple and bringing their own children here.

Some people go to the temple for the ritual observance of the festival on the day it actually appears in the calendar. But usually families come with their children on the weekend, when the social event is conveniently celebráted by all members of the ethnic group. This is the 'expressive' role of religion that Durkheim refers to when he asserts that symbolic representations are indispensable to the group. He observes that the functions performed by religion are common to all societies as there is, according to him,

no society which does not feel the need of upholding and reaffirming at regular intervals the collective sentiments and the collective ideas which make its unity and its personality. Now this moral remaking cannot be achieved except by the means of reunions, assemblies and meetings where the individuals, being closely united to one another, reaffirm in common their common sentiments (Durkheim 1915:474–5).

A festival is a time when people belonging to a common ethnic group (e.g. Telugus for Ugadi, Tamils for Pongal, etc.) unite and celebrate their common religious myths and beliefs. In the different programmes of music, dance, and drama presented on these festive occasions, religious myths and fables are explained and enacted.

Most of the parents think that once they get the children to participate in a particular social activity such as the above, they become 'involved' and understand 'our culture and traditions' much better than when they merely listen to hymns in an unfamiliar language. Meeting as families in the temple helps parents concretize abstractions about Hinduism and Indian culture that they find difficult to explain to their children at home.

The Symbolism of Ethnic Food

For many Hindu immigrants the temple has become the central site (in place of the home) for celebration of festivals, with many of their constitutive features such as rituals and traditional food. Hindu festivals in India are major events in the lives of women, who take great care to perform 'devotional' rituals authentically (Wadley 1989; Robinson 1985).[3] The different kinds of items needed for the rituals and an elaborate menu for the festival meal

[3] Although these anthropological studies are based on fieldwork in rural North India, the situation in the urban areas is not very different.

all require a great deal of planning and preparation. In traditional Hindu families in India women spend many days getting ready for these rituals. The South Indian women in Pittsburgh have told me that since they cannot celebrate festivals and share the customary meal with their extended families in India, they do so with members of their surrogate extended family in Pittsburgh (see chapter 4).

Organizing potluck lunches and dinners is one way of strengthening the surrogate extended family. Food becomes a symbol of the immigrants' shared roots (Firth 1973; Macchiwalla 1990). Ethnic food, as Kraut (1979) showed in his study of early Jewish immigrants, has historically been a distinctive feature of immigrant lives, helping to forge communal solidarity. Food plays a significant role in the lives of the immigrant Indians in my study as well. A great deal of organization is involved for providing food to hundreds of people who attend the major festivals at the temple. For instance, in November 1993 more than eight hundred and fifty people attended the *Diwali puja* (the annual 'festival of lights') and the dinner that followed. Many of my female respondents, including Shalini, Ratna, Ramani, and Lavanya, volunteered at this function, as they routinely do at others. These volunteers formulate the menu, help the temple cooks with the preparation of the food, and serve dinner to the rest of the community. Ratna said:

In India we have big families and here we are all small nuclear family units, so in the temple we are like one big extended family . . . when there is a major event like a *Diwali* dinner [in the extended family] everyone feels like being a part of it.

One cause for concern in the Indian diaspora (and in other diasporas well) is that the 'we' feeling that Ratna articulated is not entirely shared by the second generation.

Cultural Reproduction and the Socialization of Children

The anxiety over the possible assimilation of their children into American culture leads parents, especially the mothers, to make conscious efforts to socialize their children into becoming 'good Indians' or 'good Hindus'. Of course, this dilemma is shared by all ethnic groups in a pluralistic culture such as the US and many of them use religion as a means of maintaining ethnic identity

(Hammond 1988). Stephen Wieting (1975), in an examination of intergenerational patterns of religious belief speaks of

. . . the threat to society posed by the possibility that the young might not adopt the essential wisdom and values of that society. . . . If a society is to continue its existence beyond one generation, the members must transmit what they consider to be necessary knowledge and values. The continuity of a social system by definition requires transmission between generations.

My respondents have often pointed out the importance of transmitting their own religious beliefs to their children's generation. 'It is important to let them know who they are' was a common expression among the immigrants I interviewed. Fenton (1988), in his study of Asian Indians in Atlanta, found that as first generation immigrants began to realize that their return to India was unlikely, many became concerned that their children might lose contact with their heritage. Women's influence is known to be critical in the socialization of children and the Indian women in my study are no exception. It is usually the mothers rather than the fathers who bring their daughters to learn classical dance in the temple and watch them practice. Sometimes, however, when mothers are unavailable because of their jobs, the men accompany their daughters. As I will show in the next chapter, in many instances the mothers are more involved than the fathers and wield greater power in making decisions concerning their children both at home and at the temple.

Scholars of immigrant women have written positively about women's experiences in the family (Gabaccia 1991). Many western scholars, including some feminists, have difficulty in understanding immigrant women's primary identification with their families. Generalizations made about the subordinate roles of women within the patriarchal Mexican and Chicano immigrant families have been contested (Zinn 1979; Cromwell and Ruiz 1978). It is argued that the machismo philosophy that is said to characterize these families and the oppressed woman within it are stereotypes invented by 'Anglos' and perpetuated by social scientists to emphasize the 'otherness' assigned to the Mexican-American. These scholars have asserted that Mexican American women exercise considerable authority within the family and that they are active participants in decision-making.

Religiosity and Children

The women in my study consciously seek to do things as they were done by their mothers and hope that their children will do the same when they grow up. As such, they seek to establish a kind of ritual continuity with the past. Some people are confident of their ability to extend the tradition to their children's generation, but are worried about the succeeding generations. About half of my respondents admit that they themselves have become more religious after the birth of their children. Other studies on religiosity have also reported increasing levels of religious activity during childbearing years and later (e.g. Albrecht and Cornwall 1989; Bilhartz 1991). Shalini's words on this subject sum up the views of many of my respondents:

I became more devoted to the temple after my children were born. Sometimes when they want to stay at home and watch a television programme, I discourage that and push them to come to the temple . . . My parents are very religious at home [in India]. Now for *Sankranthi* I try to do everything like my mother did. I hope you understand, I do all this for my children. I find myself becoming an India-fanatic because I want my children to get exposed as much as possible to our culture. Once they are out of our culture it is very frightening to imagine what will happen. . . . I think if we take them to the temple one hundred times, at least once something might go into the child's head.

This view of the maintenance of tradition and heightened religiosity after the birth of children is mirrored in studies of other Hindu immigrant groups (Williams 1988; Clothey 1983; Saran 1985). It was a similar concern for children's religious education that made Pakistani immigrants in Great Britain participate in Islamic centres on a regular basis (Anwar 1979).

This attempt to inculcate religious values among children extends beyond mere visits to the temple and permeates many of the children's activities organized at the temple. In cultural performances such as dances and dramas, ideas are incorporated from Hindu myths and legends. For one *Sankranthi* celebration, for instance, little children dressed up as different Hindu gods and goddesses explained the religious and ritual significance of the festival. Williams sees cultural performances and instruction in ethnic dance, music, and arts as 'variations of the rituals that preserve in powerful forms elements of the religious traditions' (Williams 1988:287).

Dance as Cultural Reproduction

Indian classical dance is usually a girls' activity and it is also one of the ways in which the diasporic population constructs its identity as Hindu and Indian. *Bharata Natyam*, outside India, is synonymous with traditional Indian culture and is highly valued by expatriate Indian communities. In its modern late twentieth century manifestation, *Bharata Natyam* occupies almost the same niche that ballet occupied in the West in the nineteenth century (Leslie 1991). This Indian classical dance form has become quite popular not only among Indian immigrants but people of other cultures as well. Just as ballet has been appropriated as part of American middle class culture, it is possible that in a few decades *Bharata Natyam* will be infiltrated into the cultural milieu in the West.

In the S.V. temple a South Indian woman has been teaching *Bharata Natyam* ever since the foundation of the temple was laid. In 1991, *Kuchipudi* (another South Indian classical dance form) classes were also started in the temple. A number of young girls have been learning *Bharata Natyam* and have had their *arangetrams* (formal graduation and first public performance). About sixty students are currently learning dance in the temple. Women drive their daughters many miles to the dance classes every weekend. Some of these girls now learn *Kuchipudi* on Saturdays and *Bharata Natyam* on Sundays.

The extent of women's involvement in this activity and men's relatively low degree of involvement was amply demonstrated at a particular *arangetram* I attended at the temple. The father of the young 'graduate' appeared on the stage and said that day his wife's dream about her daughter's dance had come true. While she had been supervising their daughter's training all these years, he seemed unaware of what was going on. His lack of participation in his daughter's activity was exhibited during the reception when some members of the audience asked who that man was and why he was serving food. These people knew the girl and her mother but had seen her father for the very first time. Among other things, this is a clear acknowledgment of the critical role played by women in cultural reproduction. Thus, gendered division of labour as well as gendered socialization persist in various forms despite changes in the lives of immigrants.[4] These changes, as I will show in the

---

[4] I will examine issues of gendered socialization in terms of gender ideology

next chapter, are reflected in women assuming decision-making positions in the temple's formal organizational structure.

Organized Religious Education

Women also teach religious classes for children of different ages. Children are encouraged to read about Hinduism in the library and watch videos of Hindu mythological dramas shown recently on Indian television. Parents are obviously delighted at the children's interest in religious matters. Rajni, who works closely with children in the temple, observed:

> We have religious classes for children three years old and up. They ask a lot of questions and it is a treat to watch their eyes lighting up at the mythological stories we tell them. . . . It is so rewarding to work with these kids, it is not very ritualistic but spiritual.

However, most of my respondents think that Hindu religious education cannot be imparted in the temple alone and that they need to continue this education at home especially if they have to keep the interest of the kids. Rajni said that when she had to read bedtime stories for her daughter she consciously selected tales from the *Mahabharata* instead of *Little Red Riding Hood*. This choice can be seen as her attempt to celebrate local culture in a pluralistic society.

Almost all of my respondents have a small shrine or some space to house Hindu deities in their homes. Some of them have allotted a room for *puja* just as they do in India and have trained their daughters in lighting the lamp and other rituals. This kind of socialization is often gendered as it is the girls who are taught to be the bearers of tradition for their generation. Few boys are taught some of these traditions as their fathers themselves may not take part in many of the religious activities at home.

The S.V. temple holds Sanskrit classes every Sunday afternoon. The teacher as well as most of the students are women and it is interesting to see that they have a strong motivation to learn this classical language. Some of the women in these classes told me that they are asked a number of questions by their children about religious rituals and prayers, most of which are in Sanskrit.[5] They

---

and gendered practices in greater detail in chapter V.

[5] Sanskrit is the language of the sacred Hindu texts and scriptures, **and is no**

feel that they themselves have to be able to understand the meaning of rituals before they transmit them to their children. For some, the performance of rituals was part of their own socialization in India, but they said their participation had been merely ritualistic and the motivation to learn the meaning of many of those rituals was not very high. A few young boys and girls are also taking Sanskrit classes, although they are outnumbered by women. Hindu immigrant women have taken an active part in understanding the culture that they want to hand down to the next generation.

Finally, I must emphasize the special role of the temple as an institution in perpetuating a religious tradition in a new location. As Kim Knott in her study of Hindu temple rituals in Britain put it, religious practice in temples, whether in the form of regular rituals or annual festivals, provides 'an opportunity for the intensification of social relationships and the reinforcement of religious traditions' (Knott 1987:177). If institutionalization of tradition is not achieved, then the perpetuation of tradition would depend on the efforts of individual families. This might result in the private retention of religious values and culture, but 'it is difficult to see how Hinduism as a religious and social system would be perpetuated in an alien environment without undergoing some kind of institutionalization' (Knott 1987:178). The establishment and institutionalization of the S.V. temple is a major part of the process of identity-formation for the Hindu immigrants in Pittsburgh.

MANAGING DIFFERENCE: MULTIPLE IDENTITIES AT THE TEMPLE

One of the concerns of immigrants in general and the Hindu immigrants I have studied in particular is the issue of their identity in terms of nation, region, religion and language. Maxine Fisher's (1980) analogy of a multi-layered cake to describe multiple identities among Indian immigrants illustrates the complicated task of placing oneself in a particular group.[6] First, there is the national

---

longer in common usage in India. Many contemporary Indian languages, however, are derived from Sanskrit.

[6] Contemporary society requires that we play different roles to suit particular situations and some of us are affected by 'multiphrenia' a term Kenneth Gergen (1991) used to explain a psychological condition where an individual has many conflicting identities or selves.

identity of being an Indian. Second, the fact that these Indians are frequenting the S.V. temple shows the salience of Hindu religious identity. Third, within the nation, frequent visitors to the temple identify themselves as South Indian, which typically includes people who are originally from the four states of Andhra Pradesh, Tamil Nadu, Karnataka, and Kerala. Fourth, people from each of the four states speak four different languages — Telugu, Tamil, Kannada, and Malayalam, respectively — constituting a linguistic identity. Fifth, there is the gender identity that cuts across all the other levels of identity. Finally, like all Hindus, the Indian immigrants in my study have caste identities which are ascribed to them at birth. These different identities come into play in complex ways as the Indian immigrants interact with the outside world as well as with each other.[7]

National and Religious Identities

In spite of the seemingly confusing collage of multiple identities, different levels of identity surface in different circumstances (Barth 1969). Most of the people in my study make a conscious and deliberate attempt, in Goffman's words, to 'mark the boundaries' of ethnicity. In interacting with the wider American environment, for instance, the Indian and Hindu identities are emphasized. The idea of the nation for the immigrant does not merely denote a geographically bounded space, but is an 'ideological force' (Bhattacharjee 1992). As Bharati, a respondent, explained in her interview:

It is a question of identity. . . . I think we have to teach our children about our cultural heritage and to be proud about being what they are [i.e. Indian]. . . . It is bad not to take pride in one's heritage, particularly a rich one like ours. One cannot be an Indian outside and an American inside.

Although, as may be seen from the above, nations are often imagined as being internally homogeneous in cultural content, internal diversity of region, ethnicity, class, gender and religion are

---

[7] Although caste might well be a significant form of identity among the Indian immigrants, I do not have adequate data on how caste identity plays a role in South Indian immigrant lives in Pittsburgh. My analysis is confined largely to the first five identities described above.

celebrated (Handler 1994). Bharati and other Hindus in my study regard the temple as a manifestation of their religious aspirations and the rituals performed therein as symbolic assertions of their communal identity.

Regional and Linguistic Identities

Within the larger national and religious identities, various sub-groups construct more distinctive identities for themselves on the basis of region and language. Feelings of being South Indian as against North Indian are strong among many who frequent the S.V. temple. The boundary between the two signifies the line between inside and outside as well as feelings of 'us' and 'them'. The South Indian temple 'serves to dramatize and define key South Indian ideas concerning authority, exchange and worship' that its visitors identify with (Appadurai 1981). Symbolic of the difference between the two groups is the existence of two different Hindu temples in Pittsburgh. Speaking of the Hindu-Jain temple in Murraysville (a suburb of Pittsburgh), Revathi, a South Indian woman respondent said: 'It is a North Indian temple and we are not used to it. We cannot merge with them, as their culture is very different.'

Even within the South Indians other identities manifest them-selves in the form of language. Each subgroup like the Tamils and the Telugus mark members off from non-members both in their interactions with other temple-goers and in the organization of their cultural activities. As a Telugu-speaking person, I myself experienced this when I went to a Tamil celebration of the *Pongal* festival. Tamil subculture was asserted through language, type of food, and dress. The auditorium resonated with people speaking Tamil, men wore lungis (the traditional Tamil dress), performers on stage delivered Tamil jokes, and everyone later feasted on Tamil food. Although nobody exhibited hostile behaviour towards us, two of my Telugu friends and I felt uncomfortable. Our feel-ings of otherness and the Tamils sense of belonging seemed ini-tially puzzling.

My experience made better sense to me when I saw such par-ticularistic affiliations in the temple as 'primordial attachments' These are, according to Geertz, regional and kinship ties that include communities based on shared religion, language, and social

practices. In his attempt to conceptualize the dynamics of ethnicity, Geertz (1973:259) argued that one is bound to a community

as the result not merely of personal affection, practical necessity, common
interest, or incurred obligation, but at least in great part by virtue of
some unaccountable absolute import attributed to the very tie itself.

These primordial bonds manifested themselves in varied ways as
I observed different groups interact with each other.

During common religious and cultural events I have often heard
many Telugu women complaining that the Tamils are over-rep-
resented and wishing that there was greater solidarity among the
Telugus. Talking of the selection of little girls for a dance programme, Renu spoke disapprovingly of 'language politics':

There are a lot of politics in the temple. They were looking for more
girls to dance at the temple. When I suggested someone's name I was
asked if she was a Telugu or a Tamil. When I said she was a Tamil, the
person training them said although she does not mind, there are too
many politics to consider. She explained to me that the Kannada people
are usually with the Telugus and the Tamils are a different group with
whom they can't get along.

These differences, however, have not had a divisive effect on
the temple as a whole. People belonging to subgroups still come
together as South Indians to manage the affairs of the temple
and celebrate their diversity. One way in which this common
ground is attained is by accommodating distinctions rather than
ignoring them.

In the organization of many of the temple's religious and
cultural activities, these differences are taken into primary con-
sideration. The religious committee as well as the priests plan
the religious events for the year according to the religious calen-
dars of the four South Indian states. If a particular *puja* has to
be performed on different days for two different ethnic groups,
then the temple observes the rituals on both days according to
each group's particular traditions. As women who have worked
on the religious committee said, 'we try to please everyone.' That
same accommodative principle applies to the organization of the
activities by the temple's cultural committee as well. Special
festivals of particular ethnic groups, like the Tamils' *Pongal*
described above, are celebrated with their own cultural performances.

Gender Identity and Cultural Differences

Several women respondents suggested that the greater participation of women in the temple's organization is another reason why subgroup differences do not result in conflict. Some women told me that working together as women is enjoyable and they 'have a lot of fun'. The annual youth camp organized by the temple is usually conducted entirely by women. The members of the *Mahila Sangham* or women's organization are women from all the four South Indian states who group together in common activities. Another example of women grouping together is the organization of religious classes for children.[8] Women belonging to all four language groups have come together to conduct these classes. Gender and ethnic identities, in this case, seem to be complementary and not mutually exclusive. This issue of dual identity for 'ethnic women' is aptly summarized by Lavender (1986:x):

For many ethnic women in the United States today, the problem is not in accepting both identities, but in being able to reconcile them. For these women, neither of their identities is viewed as representing the absolute being and meaning of life. For these women, life itself is complex, and there are multiple values and reality. Some of these values and identities are conflictual, but others are complementary.

In fact, some of my female respondents seem to go beyond Lavender's observation by claiming that their common gender identity even overcomes their ethnic differences.[9]

REPRODUCTION AND TRANSFORMATION
OF GENDER ROLES AND BEHAVIOUR

There are some forms of gendered behaviour at the temple that reflect deep-rooted gender role socialization, while other forms seem to challenge traditional notions of male/female roles. The gendered socialization among the Indian immigrants is reflected most visibly in the dress code. Men have overwhelmingly adopted

[8] Muslim immigrant women in the United States have also been very active in teaching in Sunday schools and in raising funds for the establishment of mosques or religious centres (Haddad and Lummis 1987).
[9] This might be true in some instances, but during my fieldwork I have observed occasions when the linguistic identities of both men *and* women took precedence over their gender identities.

the western mode of dress, and so have boys. Since men in urban India do not often dress traditionally (in a *dhoti*, for example), the boys are not expected to either. Women and girls in India, in contrast, are usually in traditional dress, mostly saris and *salwar kameez*, and are only occasionally seen in skirts or jeans. While many Indian immigrant women might wear western dress to work, they continue to wear traditional clothes in their homes and for community gatherings. This dress code symbolizes the reality that immigrant women more then men are considered the custodians of religious and cultural tradition.

Participation in the cultural programmes seems to be gendered as well. Girls are the most active, followed by little boys, women, and men. Teenage girls are active participants while boys of the same age are hardly seen around. Explaining the differences between her son and daughter, Urmila seemed to justify the boy's relative lack of interest in cultural activities:

We try to go to dance concerts at the temple and the children come along. But, my son sometimes goes and plays with his friends. In fact, every Sunday when I take my daughter for the dance class my son comes along but plays football outside.

Sometimes when a particular performance requires both boys and girls, the latter often end up being dressed like boys. Some women told me that their children have formed friendships in the temple and these friendships are usually with children of the same gender. As Shalini, a thirty-five year old woman noted:

I have to force them to come to the temple, and once they come they don't want to go home. They have a lot of friends and love to play with them. In fact, I also made a lot of friends in the temple.

One often sees boys playing catch and girls sitting in groups in the auditorium, playing or chatting. The gendered activities of boys and girls in the temple are a reflection of their differential socialization. These findings are consistent with Fenton's (1988) study in which he found that not only do more girls than boys take part in Indian dance classes, but they also learn to perform rituals more than boys, reflecting their differential socialization.

Organization of the cultural programmes is almost exclusively done by women. Most mothers drive their children to rehearsals, help them learn their acts, make their costumes, and set the stage. Women travel long distances to the temple every week to train children for the programmes. Even though the president of the cultural committee was a man, his job was usually limited to the formal function of arranging programmes of artistes from out-of-town and making announcements on stage.

However, women have also made their presence felt in the formal organizational structure of the temple. There are women in almost all the committees and some of my respondents believe that there are less regional and linguistic politics at the temple if there are more women members. Gender identity, especially for women, seems to be an encompassing one. Many women in my study attempted to cut across linguistic, regional, and caste identities in order to participate in collective activities as women.

Gendered Spaces

Many of the women's activities are carried out in special spaces they have carved out for themselves in the temple. Although there is no place in the temple where men and women are segregated, there are informal ways in which gendered spaces are constructed. Women can express themselves freely and participate voluntarily in activities within these spaces that are exclusively theirs. Shalini, for instance, told me that she feels 'wanted' in the temple. As a mother, she watches over her children's activities, but in her own right, she is also called upon to help in the smooth functioning of the temple.

Women are often seen with other women friends in the smaller of the two auditoriums in the temple observing their daughters dance. It is their own private space within which they laugh, make fun of their husbands, complain about them to each other, and share the week's happenings. They share a common bond as mothers who want their children to be completely involved in the various cultural activities in the temple. There is a feeling of sisterhood — sharing recipes, discussing the menu for the next party, allotting tasks for the next function in the temple, discussing the latest ethnic fashions in India or exchanging video cassettes of Indian movies.

The men usually do not spend more than a few minutes in the auditorium during this period. They rarely disrupt a group of women or seek to take part in their conversations. While the men themselves use the temple for purposes of socializing with their own friends, they don't attempt to enter the exclusive female spaces. Women working in the temple's religious spaces, such as in the main worship area where they make floral garlands for the idol or fill *kumkum* packets for distribution to the devotees, have marked out distinctive nooks in which they contribute to the temple, and thereby, to the diasporic community. Similarly, the temple's kitchen is mainly a space for women volunteers despite the presence of two male cooks on the temple staff and the occasional male volunteer. In cooking and serving food from behind the kitchen counters, the women not only take part in a convivial activity with other women, but, significantly, they also get a sense of their participation in a critical temple programme, the distribution of *prasadam* (sacred food).

While the women are engaged in these activities, men proceed towards the office or in search of their own friends. They volunteer in the office, helping people buy tickets for various *pujas* or handling other organizational activities in the temple. The temple office is a space where men of different professions and those who speak different languages work together. Venugopal, one of the men I interviewed, said that the work he does in the manager's office serves as his recreation for the weekend, taking his mind off the pressures of his medical practice. He also gets satisfaction in helping people and guiding out-of-town devotees around the temple and sometimes, the city. Although some women who are on the board go into meeting rooms, they are not visible in the main office as are the men. This area is one of the exclusive male spaces in the temple.

There are conspicuous spaces such as the ones I described here which are quite gendered; these spaces are well-protected by men and women and there is little effort to encroach upon them by the opposite sex. However, there are more inconspicuous, 'invisible' spaces, especially traditionally gendered ones such as board meetings, which have been penetrated by women. Thus, while there is a certain amount of continuity of tradition, the immigrants in my study are also engaged in transforming various traditions both in the temple and in their homes.

ACCULTURATION: ACCOMMODATION AND RESISTANCE

The influences of the dominant culture on the immigrant community's adaptation process are quite substantial. Among cultural changes that could occur through acculturation are alteration of original linguistic, religious, educational and other institutions (Berry 1988). As pointed out by Pye (1979:17) in a comparative study of Christianity and Buddhism,

. . . the transmission of religion from one culture to another whether geographically or chronologically means that new cultural elements are introduced to the tradition and new demands are made upon it.

Although immigrant churches and other institutions have attempted to reproduce the traditions of the parent institutions in the home country many

. . . were not transplants of traditional institutions but communities of commitment and, therefore, arenas of change. Often founded by lay persons and always dependent on voluntary support, their structures, leadership, and liturgy had to be shaped to meet pressing human needs (Smith 1978:1178).

The temple in Pittsburgh was constructed by so-called lay people who had no training either in religious scriptures or temple rituals. Also, the physical setting itself has undergone innovations and adaptations to suit the needs of the country in which it is situated. Clothey (1983) described some of these innovations such as the use of brick and mortar instead of stone in the temple construction, the inclusion of rest rooms below the sanctuary in the same building, openness of the inner worship area to non-Hindus, use of milk in cartons, and the serving and preparation of food by non-brahmins on the temple premises. There are coke machines as well as pay phones in the temple area, adding to the non-traditional components of the traditional setting. Nevertheless, resistance to change can be seen in the fact that the sculptors were flown in from India and the installation (*pratisthapana*) of the idols (that were shipped all the way from Tirupati, India) was done strictly according to the *Vaishnava* tradition. Lynn Davidman (1991) points out in her comparative study of two Jewish Orthodox communities that many Orthodox communities can be placed along a continuum of accommodation and resistance to forces of modernity. The Hindu immigrants in Pittsburgh both accommodate forces of modernity as well as consciously resist assimilation into the dominant culture.

The processes of accommodation can be seen in the ritual sphere. The *abhishekam* (a ritual bath of the idol) of the principal deity, Lord Venkateswara, is traditionally performed in Tirupati on Saturday (the deity's auspicious day of the week). However, at the S.V. temple in Pittsburgh this *abhishekam* is performed at 11:00 a.m. on Sundays to suit the schedules of the devotees. Also, as Shalini mentioned, Christians 'go to church on Sunday and we Hindus come to the temple'. Thus, there seems to be an attempt to create an institution that is parallel to the Sunday church.[10]

Some rituals which are usually performed in the main worship area are moved to the auditorium on special festivals to accommodate more people and to avoid excessive smoke from the sacred fire near the shrine. On these occasions, many devotees sit in chairs instead of on the floor or on the carpet as is done traditionally, giving it the aura of a church or synagogue service. During one such ritual, I observed that people did not care to remove their shoes as they would have done if a *puja* was going on in the main worship area or even at the home shrine. Fenton predicts that the temples might eventually lose their distinctive character:

In America, Hindu temples tend to become like other American voluntary associations, and in time they will begin to resemble American synagogues and churches (Fenton 1988:179).

The multilingual character of the temple's visitors presents interesting dynamics in the process of accommodation. For example, English is used on some religious occasions, suggesting a transformation of traditions among the immigrants. The temple priests often use English to address an audience during collective worship sessions. Although the priests (who are conversant in most of the four South Indian languages) speak an Indian language with people they know can understand it, they make it a point to address a larger group of devotees in English. A common Hindu ritual performed by a married couple or a family is the Satyanarayana *puja* during which a priest usually narrates a mythological legend in an Indian language. At the temple the priest performs the ritual, but asks the devotees to read an English translation of the legend. One of my respondents Ujjwala said:

They do it differently from the way it is done in India. For Satyanarayana *puja* they give us the book and make us read the story [in English]. I feel

10 This is perhaps similar to some Reform Jewish temples in the late nineteenth and early twentieth centuries holding their services on Sundays as opposed to Saturdays.

good to listen to the priest saying it in Telugu even if I have heard it before a number of times. I don't get the same satisfaction when we ourselves read it.

Ujjwala's lament about the apparent weakening of tradition can, however, be offset by ample evidence of resistance to change in the temple. One example of such resistance is the recitation of hymns and prayers by the priests in Sanskrit in spite of the fact that it is an archaic language understood by few. On these occasions only a handful of devotees, who are familiar with the particular prayers, recite along with the priests. Another instance of a steadfast adherence to convention is the priests' wearing of a dhoti and a thin shawl flung over their bare chests even in winter.

In an immigrant context, adaptations and compromises in religious practices are often greater than in the country of origin. Issues of purity and pollution in traditional Hinduism are quite complex and some of the rituals cannot be strictly observed in this country. For instance, there are carpets even in the main worship area of the temple and when everyone walks on the same carpet, ritual purity becomes almost impossible to maintain.[11] One of my respondents, Sandhya says she tries hard to observe all the important rituals, but admits that it is difficult to do things exactly as they are done in India for there is 'no purity, but only pollution'. Another respondent Leela said that the family room has been converted into her puja room at home as it is the only place where 'complete purity' can be maintained without a carpet.

While Sandhya and Leela strive to resist change, some other immigrant women have compromised to the exigencies of living in another culture. One such major compromise is that some women go to the temple even while having their menstrual periods (traditionally considered a 'polluted' condition for women) as they either have to drop off their children or attend a Sanskrit class themselves. The fact that most of these women do not enter the main worship area during these visits does not preclude it from being characterized as a major form of accommodation, even as it demonstrates some resistance to change.

[11] Hindu temples traditionally are not carpeted and require worshippers to enter barefoot after having washed their feet at the entrance. Although devotees in the Pittsburgh temple take their shoes off before entering, many still keep their socks on and it is not the same as walking barefoot on a floor that is cleaned and washed daily.

On routine visits to the temple (i.e. not on festive occasions) many women wear skirts, trousers or jeans, a style of dress that is extremely rare in a temple in India. In another accommodative gesture, candy is used instead of tropical fruits for blessing children on festivals such as *Sankranthi* or *Pongal*. Often on these occasions, food is served on separate tables for adults and children keeping in view the latter's lack of enthusiasm for the traditional spicy fare. The children almost always feast on an American menu consisting of cup cakes, brownies, potato chips, french fries, macaroni and cheese, and fruit salad.

Conversations between parents and children are another indication of the acculturation process. Most parents try to talk to their children in their native language, but few children respond in that language. Parents feel that children should be able to speak in native languages at least when they go back to India and meet their grandparents. However, most children speak in English and even if they occasionally use their native language, they are self-conscious of their American accents. Rajni, who has been in Pittsburgh for over twenty-five years, told me that in her early years in this country she used to speak to her children in English out of a fear that they might not grow up speaking good English. More recently, she started regretting her early decision and has been trying consciously to make her youngest daughter learn Indian languages. A couple of women have been conducting Telugu and Tamil classes every Sunday at the temple and Rajni and many parents send their children to learn one of these languages.

These instances of accommodation and resistance, or continuity and change demonstrate, in Wuthnow's words, that

Modern religion is resilient and yet subject to cultural influences; it does not merely survive or decline, but adapts to its environment in complex ways (Wuthnow 1988:475).

Conclusion

In this chapter, I have examined the various ways in which South Indian immigrants in Pittsburgh attempt to cling on to the values of their country of origin while at the same time adapting to and accommodating some of the cultural features of the host country. They are engaged in the process of cultural *reproduction* which involves *creating* a new diasporic culture that they seek to transmit to successive generations. The Hindu immigrants grapple with different identities and the temple becomes a site on which these identities interact within the larger diasporic identity. Gender identity, especially for women, becomes an all-encompassing one as they engage in cooperative activities overcoming other identities that separate them.

As I will show in chapter IV, defying 'traditionally' defined gender roles, the South Indian immigrant women in Pittsburgh exercise their authority as legitimately elected public officials in the temple's formal organization. Far from being 'confined to the domestic sphere', women have been very much an integral part of the temple's bureaucratic structure. This kind of participation of women has resulted in the subversion of the traditional public/ private dichotomy.

IV

Gender and the Renegotiation of Public/Private Spheres

The S.V. temple is not merely a 'public' place of worship, but is a pivotal site for the renegotiation of the 'private' and the 'public' spheres by the South Indian immigrants. In this chapter, I examine the gendered nature of this renegotiation by studying the interactions and relationships of the women and men who frequent the temple. This process of redefinition by the immigrants, particularly the women, leads me to question the distinctions rendered by social science (and, probably, by traditional social norms) about the different roles played by women and men in these two domains.

FEMINIST PERSPECTIVES ON THE PUBLIC/PRIVATE DICHOTOMY

The existence of distinct public and private spheres of social life is often taken for granted in popular as well as in academic discourses, but attempts to coherently delineate those spheres are rarely made. Nevertheless, a wide array of meanings emerge from even a cursory review of how the terms 'public' and 'private' have been used in the literature. The 'public' is often associated with government, the economy, and places and issues that are accessible to a large number of people. The 'private', on the other hand, is often associated with the family or the home, sometimes with the solitary aspects of an individual's life (Keohane 1987).

In traditional social science research, women have been relegated to the private or domestic arena, while men are said to be in control of the public, i.e. of the economic, political and religious institutions. The public/private distinction has been institutionalized in liberal political thought and, as an extension, a gendered division of labour has evolved, based on an identification of the public and the private with male and female spheres, respectively. Functionalist writings, especially, have represented the public as a male preserve constituting political, administrative, and economic dimensions of life; and the private or domestic sphere, in which the functions of reproduction and nurturance are fulfilled, as the women's sphere. Parsons (1955) conceptualized basic roles in the family as 'instrumental' and 'expressive' and dichotomized them as male and female roles respectively. He said division of labour in the family was based on 'sex' and was functional for the integration of the family and for marital solidarity as it eliminated competition between husband and wife. The family as an institution would depend on this rather 'unequal' relationship between the spouses. This kind of a division between work and home, public and private, male and female, was part of the liberal tradition of which Parsons's work was a part. The United States has a philosophy of individualism but these individuals were largely male. It was only the women's suffrage movement that led to the traumatic acceptance of women as voters. Women were supposed to play the emotional functions and had to be available at their homes which were usually a good twenty miles away from the workplace. The drive from the workplace to the home was a physical separation of the 'rational' functions that men performed in the workplace to the 'emotional' time they spent at home with their 'expressive' wives. That there was unemotional, routine and often boring but essential work at home was an unrecognized factor.

An analysis of the division of social life into public and private spheres first entered feminist scholarship through cultural anthropology. In her theoretical overview to the volume, *Women, Culture and Society*, Michelle Rosaldo (1974) posited a dichotomy between domestic and public realms as a way of analysing women's positions in a wide range of historical and social settings. She stated that women's status will be lowest in those societies in which there is a firm distinction between the domestic and the public spheres, especially where women are placed under a single man's authority in the home. She further observed that when women exert significant pressures on the social life of a group, they do this through informal influence and power rather than through formal authority. To some extent, Rosaldo's essay, along with others in the above mentioned collection (Rosaldo and Lamphere 1974), reinforced the existence of the dichotomy between public and private and showed how the division of social life perpetuates the lower status of women across cultures (Fraser and Nicholson 1990:28–9). Anthropologists have noted that women in many cultures are engaged in domestic or private pursuits which absorb a very large portion of their lives, while men spend little time in these activities. Consequently, women have few opportunities to exercise their skills outside the domestic sphere of home and family.

Recently, however, a number of feminist writings have challenged this traditional dichotomy between the public and the private and the roles delegated to men and women in these domains (see, e.g. Rosaldo 1980; Sharistanian 1986, 1987; Helly and Reverby 1987). In Pateman's (1983:281) words:

The dichotomy between the private and the public is . . . ultimately what the feminist movement is all about. Although some feminists treat the dichotomy as a universal, trans-historical, and trans-cultural feature of human existence, feminist criticism is primarily directed at the separation and opposition between the public and private spheres in liberal theory and practice.

Notions of 'public' and 'private' have very different implications for the lives of men and women. Feminists have questioned the universality of the distinction between public and private spheres and, consequently, between male and female. There is considerable agreement among feminist scholars such as Nancy Fraser, Iris Young, Seyla Benhabib, and Maria Markus that the public/private dichotomy in social organization as well as in ideological debates has been quite harmful to women (Benhabib and Cornell 1987). The contemporary women's movement has made originally 'private' matters such as sexual division of labour in the family into 'public' issues of justice and asymmetrical power relations. As Seyla Benhabib (1992:110) points out, the women's movement as well as feminist scholarship in the last two decades have shown that the conventional distinction between the public and the private have been 'part of a discourse of domination which legitimates women's oppression and exploitation in the private realm'. The familiar slogan, 'the personal is the political', subverts the public/private dichotomy, and feminists who use this slogan recognize that private lives are shaped by public, political realities and that there are power dynamics that operate in the home as well as in the workplace (Keohane 1987).[1]

In a revision of her initial position discussed earlier, Rosaldo (1980) herself suggested that there are no clear distinctions between public and private, or between male and female roles within those domains. According to Rosaldo, when scholars link female lives to domestic spheres, they are interpreting sexual hierarchies in purely functionalist or psychological terms. For her, such an interpretation minimizes the significance of inequality and power. She warned against universalist assumptions about women's and men's delegation to separate spheres. Variables such as cultural identity and social class need to be considered for a complete understanding of the so-called gendered spheres. Rosaldo asserted that a

... woman's place in human social life is not in any direct sense a product of the things she does (or even less a function of what, biologically she is) but of the meaning her activities acquire through concrete social interactions. And the significances women assign to the activities of their lives are things that we can only grasp through an analysis of the relationships that women forge, the social contexts they (along with men) create — and within which they are defined (Rosaldo 1980:400).

Following Rosaldo's astute suggestion, I analyse the concrete social interactions of men and women in the S.V. temple in order to decipher the meanings they assign to their activities. It is through their concrete interactions and relationships that the South Indian immigrants redefine the cultural spaces accorded to women and men and thus the public/private dichotomy. Conventionally, temples, as religious institutions, are seen as part of the public sphere, whereas immigrants' homes are understood to be part of the private realm. Here, I show how this boundary has been blurred to a great extent by the immigrants who have made the temple the centre of their lives.

[1] According to Iris Young (1987:74), the slogan 'the personal is political' denies 'a social division between public and private spheres, with different kinds of institutions, activities and human attributes'. This slogan, for Young, implies that all institutions and practices must be within the realm of public discussion and expression and that no individuals or their actions must be confined to the private sphere.

At the S.V. temple in Pittsburgh, women and men have given prominence to those activities, such as socialization of children, which were usually considered part of the domestic sphere back in India. In this sense, the Pittsburgh temple has important elements of the private sphere within it. However, the temple is a large bureaucratic organization in which South Indian women have subverted the image of the 'male administrator' by actively contesting for electoral positions (a public activity) and assuming power in the temple's organization.

Women's Role in the Creation of a Public Religious Institution

The construction and maintenance of temples outside India is a highly visible and public assertion of religious identity by Hindu minorities in ethnically plural societies. The motivation to build the S.V. temple was at first a private desire of parents to have their daughters learn a dance form that is popular in India, but inaccessible to immigrants in the United States. It was originally a woman's (Rajni's) dream for moving away from the makeshift basement worship site to a 'real' temple that motivated the Hindu immigrant population to build the temple.[2]

Rajni in her interview, described the period as being 'very emotional' and as 'the days of *tapas* (penance)' not only for her but for the entire Indian immigrant community. It was the time when India was at war with Pakistan over the issue of Bangladesh and immigrant Indians living in the United States (which was supporting Pakistan) experienced a great deal of stress. The constant pressure to defend India's political actions helped bring the Indian immigrants together, overcoming regional and linguistic barriers among them. The sense of insecurity engendered by a tumultuous political event (the war) pushed the Hindus further into concretizing their rather abstract vision of a temple on the mountain top. During the period of revivalism and nationalism in India, there was a celebration of Indian culture which included several redefinitions of Hinduism. Similarly, during the time of political crisis in South Asia, the immigrant Hindus took on the act of temple-building. But, at the same time, this need for a public

---

[2] See chapter I for a detailed account of the temple's history.

reassertion of identity was not without a private urge to transmit cultural values to their own children. Therefore, the very establishment of this temple involved an intricate intermingling of both public and private aspects of social life.

During the arduous process of temple construction, there was a weakening of the traditional Hindu ideal that men play a predominant role in the public religious sphere while women tend to domestic religious rituals. Ever since the temple's foundation was laid, women and men participated almost equally in the public tasks of collecting funds, supervizing workers, chauffeuring the architects, sculptors, and priests, etc. Many of my respondents fondly remember the combined efforts of a number of people and do not recall any special gender dynamics that were in operation. From the early days women started assuming formal authority over the temple's organization. Rajni, for instance, told me about how, as the first treasurer of the temple, she had to drive frequently to the temple to sign cheques. Most of my respondents describe the integral role played by women in the institutionalization of the temple as a natural process ('it just happened that way'), rather than as a result of a conscious feminist move to assert themselves in traditional, male spheres.

Women's participation was not limited, however, to the establishment of the temple. As I have shown in chapter III, they continue to play a more central role in the temple's activities today. Some of my respondents said that men who were more active during the original fund-raising no longer play a significant role in the temple's activities, but many of the women continue to do so. One public aspect of the temple is the guided tours organized for groups of tourists or school and college students, generally with women serving as tour guides. Rajni, who has been doing this for a number of years, feels it is her 'duty' to educate 'outsiders' about the rich heritage of India and help establish deeper roots for Hinduism outside India. She also represented the S.V. temple at a 1991 conference at Harvard University on religious and cultural pluralism in the United States. A number of large-scale religious events in the temple are organized by committees headed by women.

This not only shows that the immigrant women in my study have successfully entered the public sphere, but also that the public face of the temple in Pittsburgh is often that of a woman. There has thus been a feminization of a religious institution. I use the term 'feminization' in the same sense that Hannah Levin (1980) uses the term 'womanization' to refer to the infusion of nurturant values into the workplace environment. I see feminization as part of a broader process of humanization of the public/private sphere (in this case, the religious institution).[3] This is largely due to structural as well as cultural changes that have occurred due to immigration. In Hindu temples in India today, rarely do we see women being permitted to assume any leadership positions. Women devotees are seen in large numbers, constituting a sizeable proportion of the laity, but the performance of religious activities continues to be predominantly a male preserve.

Women's participation in the temple activities in Pittsburgh could be partly attributed to the unavailability of adequate labour to perform the various specialized tasks associated with the organization and management of a Hindu temple in India.[4] Activities such as making garlands for the idols, taking care of the clothes and jewellery that adorn the idol constitute paid labour. In India, there are people of different classes and castes to perform these activities. The trained male priests who emigrate are primarily concerned with the performance of the rituals rather than with administrative matters. Temple administration in the diaspora is not a political activity the way it is in India where the major temples are run by bureaucratic Departments of Endowments and Executive Committees whose members are appointed by the ruling party. The needs of the diasporic community to establish its identity in an alien land require a different kind of administrative capability that educated women and men seemed to have acquired. For instance, one of the central activities of the Pittsburgh temple is to patronize other Hindu temples all over the Indian diaspora. Moreover, the immigrants find the need to present the temple as a symbol of their identity both to the host culture as well as try to attract new immigrants into becoming a part of the Indian diaspora. The upper caste male priest is no longer given the kind of central importance in the religious institution abroad and he

---

[3] I am not employing the term 'feminization' in the sense in which it has been used to refer to the 'feminization of poverty' or the 'feminization of clerical labour'. Used in this sense, it describes the structure of unequal opportunities for women and the gendered nature of the stratification system.
[4] I would like to thank Rehana Ghadially for helping me to clarify this point.

often remains confined within the temple where he performs his rituals. The priests in Pittsburgh are quite comfortable taking a back seat in the administration of the temple while the women play an active role.

However, it would be simplistic to say that women's central role in the temple is mainly due to lack of adequate labour in the diaspora. There is also a loosening of patriarchal practices both in the everyday lives of immigrants as well as in a traditionally male-dominated arena such as a religious institution which is responsible for the increased participation of women.[5]

In a study about Indian immigrants in New Jersey, Keya Ganguly (1992) argues that Indian immigrant women experience 'acute alienation' when they are outside of the domestic sphere. Ganguly says that women are comfortable within the home and even experience power, but are uncomfortable and out of place in the public sphere. Ganguly falls into the trap of dichotomizing public and private spheres instead of conceptualizing them as overlapping arenas of life. The examples of Rajni and of other women in my study challenge the image of the hapless Indian immigrant woman, devoid of all agency outside of the home, painted by Ganguly. Similarly, Anannya Bhattacharjee (1992), in an otherwise perceptive essay on the contestations of Indian identity by a South Asian women's advocacy group in New York, also tends to underestimate the significant roles played by Indian immigrant women outside the home. Resurrecting the public/private dichotomy, she describes the activities of women in the diaspora as mostly confined within the domestic sphere. As my study shows, the South Indian immigrant women in Pittsburgh have cut across this dichotomy by exerting considerable influence in the S.V. temple.

The Feminization of a Public/Private Organization

The temple has all the features of a formal organization: it has an annual income of about a million dollars a year and is governed by an elected board of directors, a board of trustees, and an executive committee. There are several other committees that plan

[5] I will discuss in detail in the next chapter the changing gender roles, ideologies and practices.

and oversee particular religious, cultural, and social activities in the temple. These boards and committees have almost equal participation by men and women. In fact, at one point in this study, there were more women than men on the board of directors, which is the main decision-making body in the temple. Far from being relegated to the domestic sphere, women have been very much an integral part of the temple's bureaucratic structure.

As far as the organizational hierarchy is concerned, there are no formal offices that are separated by gender. In 1991 the chairperson of the board was a woman, whereas in 1993 it was a man. The leadership roles occupied by South Indian women at the S.V. temple are notable in contrast to some other Indian religious communities which maintain gender hierarchies. For instance, Helen Ralston (1988) in a study of South Asian women in Canada, found the men to be the leaders and office-bearers of the religious organizations, while women were in more 'inferior' positions. The only committee at the Pittsburgh temple that was based on a gendered division of labour is the *Mahila Sangham* (women's group). In fact, one of my male respondents Satish quipped that there is no rule barring him even from the women's group. The group, however, does perform very traditional gender-specific functions. Shanta, one of my respondents, expressed her displeasure about the existence of this *Mahila Sangham* because it perpetuates traditional roles.

I don't like the *Mahila Sangham* and I have never joined it at all because the *Mahila Sangham* is always relegated to serving in the kitchen. That is not something that the men could not do. After all they have two male cooks there.

She pointed out, however, that the *Mahila Sangham* was not something imposed by the men; the women were themselves responsible for the creation of the group and most of them enjoyed participating in its activities. The initiative and agency that the women demonstrated in organizing this exclusive gendered space also resulted in their experiencing a certain degree of empowerment (see chapter III).

In the religious committee, women have been working with priests in drawing up the religious calendar of the year, something that is very rare in many Hindu temples, in India. Hindu women's role in the ritual sphere has been quite central but Bharati, another respondent, has described her participation in the temple's organization in the past few years in these words:

I was a volunteer for many years. I am now on the religious committee, education committee, construction committee, and the monetary committee. . . . Before that both me and my husband were on the cultural committee for many years. I like to take care of all these activities in my free time and I enjoy working in the temple. In the education committee we do a lot of work for organization of meditation classes and decide what lectures to have. On the religious committee, we have to find people to help during the major *pujas* and other things. During the long weekends when there are more people visiting the temple we have to see if things are running smoothly.

Although Bharati and her husband work full time in her family's business, she spends a large portion of her weekends in the temple. The wide range of work, she said, she does at the temple is typical of many of my respondents. Interestingly, she is learning a lot of new things about Hindu rituals that she would never have had the opportunity to learn had she been in India. Thus, the activities of the women in the temple are not merely an extension of the so-called domestic sphere, but they are very prominent and assertive in the public sphere as well.

While these women receive enjoyment and fulfilment by working with a close-knit group, they are extremely professional about their activities in the temple. Urmila, who at the time of the interview was the president of the executive committee, said gender was not an important variable in the leadership and larger goals of the organization:

I get along with them [male colleagues] well and I never look at people as men or women, I only see them as people working with me on the committee. We spend a lot of time deciding about what to do in the future and how to raise funds for the temple.

Thus, even as these immigrant women are celebrating 'community' through religious practice, they are involved in critical decision-making activities in the temple organization. By performing deftly in such rational bureaucratic positions these women explode the conventional myth of women being associated with 'emotional labour' (Hochschild 1983). Many of the Hindu immigrant women like Urmila, Ramani, and Bharati are highly educated and have jobs and careers of their own. But, while for these women their work in the temple's administration may mean extending their roles as professionals and businesswomen from the workplace to the temple, for others, such as Rajni and Shalini, who are primarily homemakers, the temple is the public space in which they exercise formal authority. Women's participation in the temple does not seem to be related to whether they have occupations and professions outside the home. Homemakers as well as those who work outside the home are equally vocal and devoted to their responsibilities in the temple's formal and informal organizations.

It appears that immigrant Hindu women have not only been able to penetrate into positions of power in the temple's public organizational (male) sphere, but they are also in control of the more private tasks of supervizing cultural reproduction for their children. An overwhelming number of my respondents have told me that the temple's primary role is in the perpetuation of tradition for the younger generation. In this respect, the mothers are more involved and wield greater power in making decisions concerning their children. Ratna, who at the time of our interview was the chairperson of the board of directors, commented on this aspect:

Now a lot of mothers are involved, and if there are more women on the committee then they are immediately encouraging about any programme that we want to start for children. Men do talk about it and they usually go through with it, but it is the women who show more interest. There is greater recognition of the child's needs.

Mothers are especially interested in a number of educational projects for children and take their jobs on the educational committee very seriously. There are periodic youth camps in which language and religious education is often imparted by some of the mothers. This, of course, is part of the larger process of socialization for which the mother is expected to take responsibility.

Women who are part of the Pittsburgh temple's organization have been actively trying to bring some of their private goals into the public arena. This is quite similar to women's participation in late nineteenth century women's organizations in Kansas and elsewhere (Underwood 1986; Fish 1986; Gifford 1986). Underwood points out that these organizations were 'personal' in the sense that they affirmed the women's 'sense of validity and importance of their own values'. This can be seen clearly in the history of the Women's Christian Temperance Union (WCTU) which in 1879 transformed its central goal to fighting for women's suffrage (Gifford 1986). Prominent leaders of the movement denied the separation of private and public spheres and, instead, understood the two as overlapping, suggesting that both needed reform. They saw the woman's sphere as extending out from her home to include the public arena. Women argued that if they got the right to vote, then the values of purity and piety that they promoted in the domestic sphere would be extended into the public sphere, thereby humanizing it (see Ryan 1992). A more recent, twentieth century example of women taking an active part in a public organization is among the Nizari Ismaili Muslims in North America. These Muslims, who came to the US mostly from the Indian subcontinent, have women members in their immigrant organization's religious councils (Williams 1988). Similarly, Hindu immigrants in the late twentieth century are involved in the process of institutionalizing Hindu culture and socializing children in a public temple, thereby feminizing this sphere.

The extensive participation of women in the temple organization is largely motivated by their own personal goals for the socialization of their children. Nevertheless, in this process, they have succeeded in making this agenda a central goal of the temple, which today, besides being a place of worship, is a cultural and social institution. One might argue that because women are involved in the temple's organization primarily to fulfil their socialization responsibilities, this participation is simply an extension of traditional gender roles. However, the organization of the temple itself can be seen not only as a renegotiation of this traditional division, but also as an overlapping of the so-called private and public spheres. Indeed, following Hannah Levin (1980), I suggest that women bring certain humanistic values and attributes to the public sphere that will result in its transformation. According to Levin,

The separation of domestic and public worlds has made it possible for men to feel and behave one way at work and another at home. Often the home is seen as a refuge from the competitive, aggressive values of the job. Women may not accept this split in their behaviour so easily. . . . Women will be contributing to breaking down the artificial barriers between work and home life, between head and heart, and between men and women (Levin 1980:367).

Levin argues that as women increasingly occupy positions of power in an organization, it results in the 'womanization' of the workplace and its consequent humanization. Here, I extend her argument about the workplace to a religious institution. Further, instead of merely trying to define positions of power in the same manner as men, women have creatively introduced patterns of behaviour and emotionality that were previously confined to the domestic sphere. Drawing on a study conducted with Hungarian women engineers, Maria Markus (1986) sees a future reconstitution of the so-called public sphere as a 'potential civil society' where there is greater commitment to equality, plurality and democratic forms. Similarly, placing their private concerns about cultural reproduction and socialization of children at the centre of the temple's agenda, the South Indian immigrant women in my study have merged the so-called public and private spheres and feminized this public institution.

This feminization of the temple also challenges Rosaldo's (1974) earlier assertion that when women exert pressure on a social group, it is usually through informal channels, rather than by wielding formal authority. The women in the Pittsburgh Indian diaspora exert power not only informally through small groups, but also as legitimately elected public officials in the temple's formal organization. They have wielded this influence not in a neutral way, but have used it actively to imbue a Hindu temple (a public sphere in which their role has traditionally been minimal) with features of the private realm. I do not want to give the impression here that men play a negligible part in the temple's activities. Many men have prominent roles in the temple's organization and activities. Nevertheless, they have also accepted and encouraged the feminization of the temple.

Ann Douglas, in her macro-level study of nineteenth century America, *The Feminization of American Culture*, contends that 'feminization' resulted only in the continuation of male hegemony in different guises (Douglas 1977:13).[6] The infusion of sentimental values in society and the 'feminizing' of culture did not necessarily end patriarchal values. The feminization of the religious

[6] For Douglas, 'feminization' has a negative connotation and describes what she sees as a decline in American values. I do not wish to convey that sense about the consequences of feminization for the S.V. temple and the South Indian community in Pittsburgh.

institution in Pittsburgh might also mean the perpetuation of male hegemony in different forms to some extent. For example, women continue to cook and serve food at the temple for festivals. But, many of my respondents (both male and female) have repeatedly expressed their feelings that immigrant women enjoy a more respectable position than do women back home.[7]

Social Bases of Immigrant Women's Autonomy

If the South Indian immigrant women in my study perceive a sense of greater autonomy in the US, the question is: what are the social bases of such perceptions of freedom? For most of my female respondents, the constraints and pressures of the actual extended family life (the patriarchal Indian 'joint' family in which the husband's parents, especially the mother-in-law, play an authoritative role) are absent in this country and they are able to assert greater autonomy. Even in wealthy families in India, some of these women did not have economic control and they had to live in the shadow of the mother-in-law. A woman was able to exert her autonomy only as a mother of a son.

Parents of some of the Indian immigrants have followed them to the US, but they are dependent financially as well as physically to a large extent on their daughters or daughters-in-law. They, therefore, cannot exercise the same kind of authority over the female members of the family as they could back home. The life of an Indian homemaker in the US is comparable to the urban homemaker in India in many respects, but unlike her counterpart she has greater mobility and freedom.

My study also reveals that this sense of greater gender equality has, to a large extent, evolved through the mediation of the community's cultural life revolving around the temple in Pittsburgh. And, it is the particular class situation that allows the immigrants to give primacy to cultural issues. Following Rosaldo's (1974) recommendation, variables such as social class and inequality need to be considered in order to gain a better understanding of gender in the context of the public and the private.

In her study of Korean immigrant women in Hawaii, Chai (1987) says that women in the Korean diaspora are engaged in

---

[7] The contradictions between gender ideology and practice among the Hindu immigrants in my study will be discussed in chapter V.

paid labour. Their economic contributions to the home lead to more egalitarian gender relations. The economic constraints on the community members and the compulsion for both spouses to work in menial jobs gives women more power in the private sphere (home) and in the immigrant community. Chai's analysis that egalitarian gender relations emerge out of economic constraints does not stand for the immigrants in my study. Most of them are well-established professionals and live, at least, an upper-middle class life. Many of the women work outside the home, either full-time or part-time. They feel they have attained greater status and independence in the domestic domain after immigration.

The economic security of the 'Indian immigrant bourgeoisie' (Bhattacharjee 1992) and their relatively higher class position enabled this immigrant group as a whole to focus on cultural issues. Hindu immigrants in many parts of the world could afford to pool massive resources to construct the community's cultural identity through religious institutions. Once a religious institution was established in Pittsburgh (and, as I explained earlier, even during the planning stages), women played a prominent role and, eventually, what has traditionally been known as the women's exclusive agenda (nurturance and socialization of children) has become the central goal of the temple. It is, perhaps through this process that South Indian women in Pittsburgh have gained greater respect and equality. It is not economic insecurity, but economic security combined with the blurring of the public/private spheres that has led to the empowerment of these women.

The Temple as a Private Sphere: The Surrogate Extended Family

The renegotiation of the temple as a public/private sphere discussed above takes place within a context in which Indian immigrants, actively and self-consciously, celebrate their community. Vishnuvardhan, one of the male members of the temple board, said that his personal goal is to develop the temple into a larger cultural and social centre.

It is mainly to preserve our own culture, particularly when you have the second generation growing up here. The only thing they know about India is what we talk about and what they see when they go to India. So I think we have to create an atmosphere that this culture is natural, it is normal. The children are spending about forty hours a week in school and are completely influenced by that culture. So, I think the temple should provide a means of showing them our own unique culture.

Rajaraman, who describes himself as extremely religious, said he began to regularly attend the temple only after his daughter started taking dance lessons there.[8] Both men and women who are active in the temple are extremely concerned about the socialization of their children. Although it is mostly women who actually initiate and carry out the socialization programmes for their children, men play no small part. During the organization of musical events, both men and women who are trained in Indian classical music teach songs and hymns to children. The significant point here is that socialization of children which has been considered the major responsibility of the domestic domain has been extended to the temple. In the absence of schools which impart culturally relevant education to the Indian-American children, the temple in an immigrant setting plays a critical role.

The observance of ethnic festivals is both an important feature of the children's socialization and a way for the adults to celebrate community. Many of the respondents in my study have substituted the temple as the hub of festival activity instead of the home, which traditionally served this purpose. For most Hindus in India religious events and the celebration of festivals are private affairs that take place in the homes of one of the extended family members. However, as immigrants cannot celebrate festivals with members of the extended family, the temple becomes a site for such celebrations.

Regular visitors to the temple act like members of a surrogate extended family to each other, as they want to be among friends with whom they share ethnic and religious roots. Ramani said that her family usually goes to the temple for most festivals and does not feel the need to celebrate the festivals at home. As she put it:

The doors [to the temple] are always open, and you feel homely [sic] because it does not belong to anybody, it belongs to our people. It is like a second home. . . . If we don't come for a while then my husband and I feel very depressed.

[8] A devout Hindu's religiosity is not necessarily measured by his or her temple-going. Even an extremely religious person can go to the temple very few times. In the US, however, the temple is not only a place of worship, but almost a substitute for the large extended family gathering.

Ramani and her husband are active in many of the cultural programmes that take place at the temple. It is in the ethnic celebrations that one can see most prominently the public/private nature
of temple activities for the immigrants who frequent it.

A festival is a time when immigrants belonging to a particular
ethnic group (e.g. *Ugadi* for Telugus, *Pongal* for Tamils, etc.)
unite and celebrate their common religious myths and beliefs. In
various programmes of music, dance and drama presented on
these festive occasions, religious myths and fables are explained
and enacted. Ethnic subcultures are reasserted through language,
type of food, dress and other regional distinctions. Although the
temple is technically a public place of worship, there is an ex-
clusivity that makes it no different from a private function that
may be taking place in a home. Women assume leadership roles
in the organization of these festivals as part of the community-
building process. Many of my respondents, like individuals in
other ethnic/religious groups, state that they derive a sense of
belonging through involvement in such group activities.

Many people developed a special bond with the temple as they
continued to live in Pittsburgh for a long period of time. Many
women, men and children spend a great amount of time in the
temple; it is for them a second 'home', rather than just a public
place of worship. On weekends a visit to the temple becomes a
family outing for many immigrants. This special relationship
between the temple and its visitors seems to have evolved gradually. One of my respondents, thirty year old Revathi, said that when
she first saw the temple she found it too quiet and peaceful,
especially in comparison with its parent temple in Tirupati. But
over the three years that Revathi has been living in Pittsburgh,
she said she has developed an attachment to the deity and the
temple. Unlike the mostly impersonal services available in large
temples in India, the priests at the S.V. temple give personal
attention to the devotees, taking care to make them feel at home.
As Revathi put it,

Now I am so used to the place that I am attached to it. We feel that it is
our temple because of the personal attention we get. Now if I go back to
Tirupati I may not like it. I don't even remember the deity in the Tirupati
temple. I think he looks like the one here. I relate to this temple as my
own. Here we participate in so many activities. The priests are very nice
here. Even if they are very busy they try to talk to us for a few seconds.

A couple of other respondents expressed similar feelings about participation in the temple. They feel that instead of merely being passive 'visitors' to the temple, they are active participants. As part of a minority group which is in the process of creating a community, they feel the need to stay closer to this temple much more than they would have if they were not immigrants. Shalini said that her husband had given up lucrative job offers in other places because he wanted to be close to the temple.

Many Hindu prenatal or postnatal rituals that are usually performed at home now take place in the temple. As part of a minority group which is in the process of creating a *Gemeinschaft* within a large *Gesellschaft*, the Hindu immigrants consciously create this surrogate extended family in the temple. They feel they 'belong' in this temple more than they would in temples 'back home'. In India they feel insignificant among the millions of Hindus in the many temples which are public places of worship. Moreover, they would like to see their children feeling at home in the temple in the same way that they do. One of my respondents, Ratna said:

The other day I was very happy when a girl who grew up here, came from Yale (where she studies now) with her friends and showed them around the temple. She said that she wanted them to see the temple and she felt it was her temple. That makes it nice.

This 'homecoming' of a teenager seems particularly gratifying to the first generation immigrants for whom socialization of children into an 'Indian culture' is a major goal. Many parents say that going to the temple establishes for their children some roots within the traditional culture. When they see the children identifying with the temple, it makes them happy.

The Hindu immigrant women in Pittsburgh, like women in most cultures, carry on the work of maintaining extended kinship networks. In a perceptive analysis of 'kinwork', Micaela di Leonardo (1987) argues that by separating women's participation in the labour force from their work as network organizers one gains only a fragmented understanding of women's activities. Leonardo attempts to fuse the domestic network and labour perspectives by describing Italian-American women as 'kin workers' engaged in the 'work of kinship'. She urges us to see women's roles in building and maintaining kinship relations as

the products of conscious strategy, as crucial to the functioning of kinship systems, as sources of women's autonomous power and possible primary sites of emotional fulfilment, and, at times, as the vehicles for actual survival and/or political resistance (Leonardo 1987:441).

Women in my study play a key role in the establishment and smooth functioning of social networks among the Indian immigrant community. They break down private/public barriers by institutionalizing these fictive kinship networks in the temple. In fact, these Hindu immigrant women in Pittsburgh are in control of almost all the tasks involved in network building for their families and for their community. Again, it could be argued that this is part of the perpetuation of gender division of labour within the family and the household.

However, in her study of Bengali immigrants in New Jersey, Ganguly suggests that her female informants experienced a loss of influence which they had enjoyed in India. She says that they had wielded such influence by primarily maintaining social networks and familial connections. In the diasporic context, the women 'find themselves alone and without the support systems' that provided them 'emotional and psychic sustenance' (Ganguly 1992:42). Similarly, in another study of a Bengali immigrant group in New Jersey, Sathi Dasgupta (1989) asserts that the female world is 'lost forever' to the women. According to her,

The Indian immigrant women cannot form a female world composed of other Indian immigrant women in the American society because significant kin are absent from the American society. [T]he close friends with whom the Indian immigrant women grew up, are absent from the American society. Marriage has disrupted their world of interpersonal relationships (Dasgupta 1989:141).

The observations made by the above studies of Bengali immigrants are quite different from my findings about the South Indian immigrants in Pittsburgh. Ganguly (1992:43) herself cautions that her analysis of the Bengali community is culturally specific and is not generalizable to all the diverse ethnic groups from the Indian subcontinent. The South Indian women in my study, as pointed out earlier, not only continue to build and maintain social networks, but also reconstruct an intimate 'female world' in the immigrant context. While Dasgupta might be right about the absence of kin and old friends in the American society, many of my respondents have established surrogate kin networks.

This is apart from the fact that some of them actually have siblings and other family members in different parts of the US with whom they maintain regular contacts.

Moreover, the surrogate family networks established by the women do not merely serve to extend, as some might argue, their roles in the private sphere. Among the Indian immigrants in Pittsburgh, these relationships often constitute the foundation on which various public activities are carried out. For example, in 1992, as an overt public assertion of their 'national' identity, the Indian immigrants in Pittsburgh came together in an effort to endow an Indian Nationality Room in the University of Pittsburgh's Cathedral of Learning. The extensive networks already in place were activated as a number of women joined forces in fund-raising committees and organized special events for the purpose. Another instance of how the private networks are used for activities in the public sphere is the attempt by one prominent female member of the community to organize an awareness and fund-raising group to promote literacy in rural India. This group developed mainly through the initiative of this woman and her circle of friends connected with the temple.

CONCLUSION

The differentiation of the temple as public and the home as private does not apply to the Hindu immigrants in my study. Clearly, one can see aspects of both spheres in the temple's activities. In terms of gender dynamics, the traditional division between women as the primary agents of socialization and men as the controllers of the economy and polity is challenged. Men have also been heading the cultural committee that oversees all the socialization programmes. Women, on the other hand, have not only been an integral part of cultural committees, but have also acted as treasurers and chairs of fund-raising which would traditionally be seen as those activities that exclusively belong to the male sphere.

In renegotiating the distinction between public and private spheres, the immigrant women have also challenged traditional gender roles. Women have been an integral part of every aspect of the temple right from its conception almost two decades ago. From the act of establishing this public religious institution in a pluralistic society to a gradual feminization of its activities, there has been a breakdown of separate, distinct spheres, both in terms of public/private and the gendered roles that are said to be part of these spheres. Finally, in Rosaldo's (1974:36) words:

. . . perhaps the most egalitarian societies are the ones in which public and domestic spheres are only weakly differentiated, where neither sex claims much authority and the focus of social life itself is the home.

In the Hindu immigrant context in Pittsburgh, however, the focus of social life is not the home but the temple, where the immigrants seem to be involved in not only cutting across the public and private distinctions, but also in challenging gender roles within those spheres. There is no obvious gender hierarchy within the temple organization, and almost all my respondents, both male and female, vehemently stated that there are no great inequalities among them. However, they seemed to have strongly internalized 'traditional' values and norms with regard to a woman's role within the family and other cultural institutions. This can be seen in the role played by women in cultural reproduction and socialization of children.

It is not difficult to reconcile this seeming contradiction if one understands that the extensive participation of women in the temple organization is largely motivated by their own personal goals for the socialization of their children. There is no strikingly obvious trend either towards complete egalitarianism or the complete perpetuation of traditional gender roles. In order to explicate these gender dynamics, I will examine, in the next chapter, the immigrants' gender ideologies and the strategies they employ in order to reconcile these ideologies.

V

Gender Ideologies
and Practices

In chapter III, I have suggested that some of the cultural practices that are being reproduced in the diaspora, such as classical dance, continue to be quite traditional and gendered. However, in chapter IV, I have discussed how the Hindu immigrants in my study have renegotiated the public and private spheres in the temple, leading to greater gender equality. Within this immigrant community, there is no visible trend either toward complete egalitarianism or toward the perpetuation of traditional patriarchy. In this chapter, I describe and analyse the varied gender ideologies that co-exist among the immigrants and relate those ideologies to actual behaviour patterns. An important part of this chapter is devoted to elucidating the cultural sources of the gender ideologies of the Indian immigrants. An understanding of these ideologies and the gaps between ideology and practice will help clarify the direction of changes in gender dynamics. In order to gain such an understanding, I go beyond the immigrants' activities at the temple and probe their attitudes toward various aspects of domestic life. This analysis assumes significance in the context of the feminist rejection of the public/private dichotomy where ideologies and attitudes characterizing one sphere are held to be distinct and separate from those of the other. As an experiential study of the everyday lives of women in the Pittsburgh Indian diaspora, it is essential that I make an attempt to understand the lives of these women within the context of the family as an institution. This analysis of gender ideologies and practices within the family location will help in gaining a better understanding of the role played by the women in the temple, which they have constructed as a surrogate extended family.

As I have shown in chapter III, gendered behaviour among the immigrants is rooted in the ideology that they have carried with them to the new society. When the patriarchal gender ideology predominant in Indian social life has been internalized by the immigrants, there is a tendency to conform to the norms that are associated with that ideology. Even though many of the Indian immigrant women have made inroads into male-dominated occupations, their primary identification is with their own families.

Donna Gabaccia (1991) points out that immigrant women in most cultures generally identify with their families and communities and do not think of themselves primarily as individuals. There is a tendency on the part of many Western feminist scholars to assume that once women identify with their families they are left with little or no power. Gabaccia warns that many Western feminists' tendency to dismiss massive evidence of immigrant women's identification with their families as 'false consciousness' makes them ignore the roots of feminist consciousness in other societies. Although Hindu immigrant women in the late twentieth century are not mainly confined to the domestic sphere as were Jewish immigrant women in the early parts of the century in the United States, they too identify with their families and define themselves according to traditional value systems into which they were socialized prior to immigration.

However, this does not necessarily mean that immigrant women are continuing to lead an existence that keeps them within the clutches of traditional patriarchy. Sydney Stahl Weinberg (1988:xx) notes that early Jewish immigrant women 'sought and found meaning for their lives within the framework of their own system of values and culture'. Similarly, the women in my study find empowerment within the very traditional structures of patriarchy which they subtly change in the immigrant context. I am not forwarding the proposition that there is some kind of a 'feminist movement' among the South Indian immigrants. I am merely attempting to gain some understanding of the gender consciousness of these immigrants through their own reflections on life in the US and the comparisons they make with life back in India. When immigrants begin to live in a new society and imbibe that society's values and norms through acculturation, the dominant ideology carried from their countries of origin undergoes a transformation.

In this chapter, using an analytical framework borrowed from Arlie Hochschild (1989), I first map out the varied gender ideologies and practices among the respondents and then attempt to account for such variations in ideology by examining both traditional cultural texts as well as more contemporary social trends in India.

TYPOLOGY OF GENDER IDEOLOGIES AND PRACTICES

In order to examine the gender ideologies of the Hindu immigrants and analyse how their gender strategies and practices are often at variance with their ideologies, I have adopted the conceptual framework used by Arlie Hochschild in *The Second Shift* (1989).[1] The ways in which people reconcile their gender ideology with their actual behaviour is what Hochschild calls a 'gender strategy'.

A gender strategy is a plan of action through which a person tries to solve problems at hand, given the cultural notions of gender at play. To pursue a gender strategy, a man draws on beliefs about manhood and womanhood, beliefs that are forged in early childhood and thus anchored to deep emotions. He makes a connection between how he thinks about his manhood, what he feels about it, and what he does. It is the same way for a woman (Hochschild 1989:15).

Hochschild divides the ideologies of marital roles into 'traditional', 'transitional', and 'egalitarian'. A woman with a 'traditional' ideology is described as someone who identifies more with her home than the workplace; and a man with a similar ideology would be one whose primary identification is with his work rather than with his home and family. Such a woman wants less power than her husband and is willing to make him feel that he is the boss. A person with an 'egalitarian' ideology is one who identifies with the same spheres as his or her spouse and wants equal power in the marriage. A person with a 'transitional' ideology seeks a blending of the two ideologies and identifies with both the public as well as the domestic spheres. The 'transitional' woman, unlike the 'traditional' woman, identifies with her role in the workplace as well as at home. But, unlike the 'egalitarian' woman, she expects her husband to focus on

---

[1] Hochschild's study is about housework and the gendered division of labour within the family. Although my study is not limited to housework, this framework can be gainfully employed to understand gender ideologies and practices more broadly.

bringing home a regular salary rather than on caring for the home. Most of the couples interviewed by Hochschild adhered to a transitional ideology. However, there were contradictions between what people said about their ideology and what they actually felt and did.

Hochschild's typology of ideologies can be applied broadly to the South Indian immigrants in my study, but with the understanding that there are cultural factors that make the experiences of the Hindu immigrants quite distinct from Hochschild's respondents.[2] A second, and broader, qualifier to my adoption of Hochschild's typology is that it is being used only as a valuable heuristic tool and not to precisely label each of my respondents as 'traditional', 'transitional', or 'egalitarian' women and men. I do not use these labels to classify individuals, but to describe the ideas they espouse. Further, even when used to describe ideas, these different types of ideology should be seen only as tendencies rather than as rigid categories. Such a categorization is confounded by the reality of people espousing different ideologies for different aspects of life. For instance, a particular respondent who articulates an egalitarian ideology with respect to domestic work and marital roles, supports a traditional ideology with regard to the socialization of male and female children.

Among my respondents, there are contradictions between the gender ideologies they articulate and their actual practices, as there were among those in Hochschild's study. But, more significantly, as I sought to apply Hochschild's typology beyond marital roles, I discovered that individuals in my study did not necessarily have a uniform ideological position towards all aspects of life. I present the ideologies and practices of the South Indian immigrants in my study with respect to two central areas of their lives: marital roles and aspirations for their children.

IDEOLOGIES OF MARITAL ROLES AMONG SOUTH INDIAN IMMIGRANTS

I will characterize immigrants as tending toward a 'traditional' ideology with regard to marital roles if they espouse patriarchal

[2] Hochschild's study included dual-earner couples, most of them middle class, their friends, neighbours, day care workers and babysitters in the Berkeley, California area. The immigrants in my study can be broadly characterized as middle and upper-middle class, but they have been socialized in a different cultural milieu.

beliefs and feel that men should have greater power than women. 'Traditional' practices would be a translation of this ideology into actions such as men having greater power in decision-making over household finances, and adopting a rigidly gendered division of labour at home. Those with a 'transitional' ideology of marital roles lean toward gender equality, but accept the fact that men could have greater power than women. Those couples adhering to this ideology share in the decision-making, but ultimately it is the woman who is primarily responsible for childcare and household chores. Finally, those who espouse an 'egalitarian' ideology are those who tend to believe in equality in all spheres. 'Egalitarian' practices would include sharing in decision-making as well as in housework and childcare equally.

Among the forty immigrants I interviewed, sixteen articulated a traditional gender ideology with respect to marital roles. Interestingly, an equal proportion of the men (six out of fifteen) and women (ten out of twenty-five) interviewed subscribed to such an ideology. An equal number of women and about a third of the men also had a transitional ideology of marital roles. Only nine out of the forty respondents espoused an egalitarian ideology, with a slightly greater proportion of men than women identifying with it. However, like in Hochschild's study, there is a clear discrepancy between the respondents' stated ideological positions and their practices. Based on my observations as well as interviews, it seems that only about a quarter of the sixteen respondents with a traditional ideology actually engaged in traditional practices. In fact, about half of my respondents with varied ideologies follow transitional practices (see Table 1).

TABLE 1
IDEOLOGIES AND PRACTICES OF
RESPONDENTS WITH RESPECT TO MARITAL ROLES

	Ideology			
Practice	*Traditional*	*Transitional*	*Egalitarian*	*N*
Traditional	4	4	0	8
Transitional	7	8	5	20
Egalitarian	5	3	4	12
N	16	15	9	40

Having given this overall picture of my respondents' ideologies of marital roles and practices, I will show how these dynamics between ideology and practice are played out in their lives.

Domestic Division of Labour

Eight of the forty respondents (four couples), especially those who are in upper-middle class, dual-career households, employ domestic help on a regular basis as they would have done in India. In addition, there are ten other respondents (five couples) who hire help occasionally. But unlike their counterparts in India, the Indian immigrant women are not solely responsible for supervizing household help since both spouses share the task. In India women rely on domestic help as well as on relatives rather than expect the men to become involved in these activities (Sekaran 1992). In my study, however, many of the spouses of women with demanding careers are involved in managing the household and taking care of children. As a result, one can see men with traditional or transitional ideologies participate in an egalitarian domestic division of labour. Two of my women respondents, Satya and Praveena, who are doctors, said that their husbands are primarily responsible for driving their children to dance and religious classes at the temple and contribute to household tasks.

Eleven of the fifteen immigrant men I interviewed share domestic work and attribute this to the fact that in India there is easier and cheaper access to domestic help, while in the US their wives cannot do everything on their own without the men's 'help'.[3] Secondly, the use of electrical appliances redefines the nature of household work and the men with traditional gender ideologies do not consider running the vacuum cleaner a taboo.[4] However, a majority of the men who do share domestic labour still tend to characterize their part of the work as only assisting the women, thereby reinforcing the idea that transitional or egalitarian practices need not necessarily suggest a corresponding ideology. For

[3] I did not measure the actual number of hours that each of the husbands and wives put into household work, like Hochschild did. While her study centred around housework, it is only one of the ways I have tried to understand any existing gaps between gender ideology and practice.

[4] In a traditional Hindu home it is considered ill-fortune to have the 'master of the house' even touch a broom, let alone use it.

instance, Arun, a fifty year old scientist, describes his part at home in these words:

I have accepted some changes willingly or unwillingly, and I am aware of these changes. My wife started working also and I cannot expect the same kind of service [as] from the non-working wife. If she is cooking, I wash the dishes or cut the vegetables or some other kind of help. I kind of share the responsibility.

Arun's ideology is thus traditional, while his practices are egalitarian.

Freedom and Conformity

About twenty out of twenty-five Indian women I interviewed in Pittsburgh had either traditional or transitional ideologies. They tended to advocate patriarchal values and acknowledged the superior role of the man in a marriage. However, their practices were not all traditional. In fact, many of them expressed the feeling that they enjoyed greater freedom after immigration.

For thirty-five year old Shalini, who came to the US as a new bride at the age of nineteen, life as a homemaker in the US has been quite an empowering experience. By driving to the temple, about forty miles away from her suburban home, three times a week, she has reached out to the South Indian immigrants and is an integral part of this group. She said that she is independent without the constraints of living in an extended family with her mother-in-law and other relatives. In India, women's lives in a typical patriarchal extended family are quite constrained and their position is low in the domestic power hierarchy. Shalini feels that in India she would not have had the freedom to play tennis, avoid cooking when she was not 'in the mood', or socialize to the extent that she is now used to in the United States.

Forty-eight year old Shanta, who works in a hospital, was one of the women who said she felt more 'liberated' after coming to the US She said she was now quite 'adventurous'.

I was raised to think that I will grow up, have kids, be a wife, a housewife, a mother. When I first came here, I took up a job because it was an economic necessity but later I began to like it and enjoyed being with company. There have been seventy-five per cent changes in my life after coming here. If I had stayed in India I would have slowly become a housewife as my mother did, and not do any of the things I do now. I go on holidays all over the world on my own. . . . Also I must say that Arun is quite good in *allowing* [emphasis mine] me to go on these trips.

From the above, it is obvious that some of my respondents attribute changes in their attitudes and behaviour to immigration to the United States. Shanta, for instance, had not visualized having a career and being economically independent while she was in India.

Thirty-seven year old Anita, who came to the US fifteen years ago and works as a computer programmer, said she also started experiencing, like Shanta, a sense of 'liberation' after coming to the United States. If she had lived in an extended family in India she would not have had the autonomy which she has as an immigrant. This autonomy is particularly evident for her in the performance of religious rituals.

I enjoy religion here more because I have greater freedom. In India, it becomes a ritual, you do it only because you *have* to, here you do it because you *want* to. There, I have to get up early and do all the things that our mothers used to do and then feed everyone. Here, I can wake up at nine and still do the *puja* and I enjoy the flexibility.

She feels more in control of her home in the US and experiences a sense of empowerment. From my observations of Anita's family on different occasions, Anita and her husband, forty-three year old Satish, seem to have adopted egalitarian practices. In her interview, however, Anita gave me the impression that her autonomy in the decision-making process was because of her husband's 'broad-mindedness'.

I don't feel that my role is less or his role is more, because of the equal opportunity that *he gives me* [emphasis mine]. . . . he gives me the opportunity to decide for myself and that is how I have become very confident.

In spite of their egalitarian practices, the traditional ideology of both Shanta and Anita is obvious when they describe the power hierarchy in the household. Their respective spouses 'allow' them to do certain things and 'give' them the opportunities. Espousing a traditional ideology is a common gender strategy adopted by many Indian women even when power and control within the family are more or less equitably distributed. This is quite similar to some of Hochschild's couples who have a traditional ideology but maintain egalitarian practices. Many of the Indian women in my study seem to feel that they should not give people in the community the impression that they are the ones in control. They feel that a man who is 'dominated' by his wife is not a respected member of the community. But it will be a mistake to assume that all those women who have traditional ideologies follow egalitarian practices or that they are entirely content with their life situation.

Traditional Ideology and its Discontents

Ten of the twenty-five female respondents I interviewed are home-makers, out of whom three have previously been students in the US. All of the homemakers as well as over half of those who work outside the home have traditional or transitional ideologies with respect to male and female roles within the family. However, while homemakers tend to have traditional or transitional practices, more women who work outside tend to have egalitarian practices.

Most of the immigrant homemakers I interviewed take care of almost all the chores themselves. They have a clear sense of the gendered division of labour — the women took care of the home, while the men earned their living. When some of the homemakers go to India for a long vacation, they cook and freeze food for their husbands who 'cannot' cook for themselves and do not like to eat out. Some male and female respondents also felt that women, both homemakers and those who have jobs, do more work outside the home when compared with their lives back in India. They drive their kids to school, to the temple for dance and music classes, or for piano and ballet lessons and other activities.

Thirty-five year old Lavanya, one of the homemakers I interviewed, considers her upbringing to have been extremely traditional. Her gender ideology is traditional and so is her practice. She said that once a woman is married then 'we (women) do whatever they (men) want us to do'. She wants her daughter to be raised as a 'proper' Indian girl and even observed the traditional puberty rituals for her.[5] These rituals, primarily because of the

[5] For example, among the Telugus, when a girl reaches puberty (soon after her first period) the occasion is observed as a rite of passage. She is considered to have 'matured' (*Pedda Manishi* in Telugu literally means a 'grown-up'). Female relatives and friends are invited to the girl's home to perform the ritual.

acute embarrassment they cause to the girls involved, have been given up not only by most immigrants, but also by many families in urban India.

Lavanya attributed her active participation in the temple to her husband's motivation. It was apparent to me that she had a number of friends and was active in the social circle in Pittsburgh, and it was not entirely on her husband's initiative that she came to be an important part of the Indian community. But Lavanya was modest and unwilling to admit in the interview that she has a primary role to play in determining her family's collective activities and reiterated that she merely followed her husband's wishes. She preferred to be seen as a follower of her husband rather than as someone who is an initiator.

However, Lavanya did admit to experiencing some uneasiness with her situation as she ends up taking care of her home almost single-handedly without much help from her husband. She said that she would have liked her husband to take care of some of the chores or at least offer her a glass of water when she was tired. She said that before she got her driver's license, her husband would do grocery shopping and chauffeur the kids but that changed after she learned how to drive. Once she started driving she became responsible for not only the work at home but, like many American homemakers, also for things outside the home.

Although driving allowed immigrant women to become more independent of their spouses, it made them fall into another form of gendered labour, one in which many American women are already embedded. Immigrant women's ability to drive brings with it additional responsibilities associated with the traditional home-maker role in the US, such as shopping for the home and driving children around. Lavanya's attitude might seem to be in complete harmony with her socialization, but her immigrant situation made her share some of the additional burdens that American home-makers experience.

A male respondent, Satish, said that immigrant Indian women are burdened with responsibilities outside the home that the men usually took care of in India. According to Satish, the women are actually doing more work (like taking care of bills and insurance problems) which in India were part of the man's contribution to the home. There is thus the danger of falling into the 'breadwin-ner/homemaker' trap of the industrialized world (Davis 1988). So changes have not necessarily been totally liberating for the Indian immigrant women and there is the danger of falling from one kind of subjugation and dominance into another.

These ideologies of marital roles articulated by my respondents are only to a small extent reflected in their aspirations for their children and the way they socialize them. Whatever their beliefs may be with respect to the position of women and men in a marriage, they don't necessarily seem to apply the same standards to their daughters and sons.

GENDER IDEOLOGIES IN ASPIRATIONS FOR CHILDREN

I will characterize the immigrants in my study as tending toward a 'traditional' gender ideology with respect to the aspirations they have for their children if they have differing expectations for their male and female children. Parents according greater priority to the education of a son over that of a daughter is an example of 'traditional' gendered practice. Those with a 'transitional' gender ideology with respect to their children believe in gender equality, but have greater expectations for a son's success than that of a daughter. Parents who get both their sons and daughters educated, but seek to channel their sons' energies toward a professional career while they encourage their daughters to settle for more 'feminine' occupations are engaged in transitional practices. An egalitarian gender ideology in this case would be a belief in gender equality for their children in all areas of life. Such an ideology is reflected in practices such as providing boys and girls equal opportunities to pursue career goals.

TABLE 2
GENDER IDEOLOGIES AND PRACTICES OF RESPONDENTS WITH RESPECT TO ASPIRATIONS FOR CHILDREN

	Ideology			
Practice	*Traditional*	*Transitional*	*Egalitarian*	*N*
Traditional	0	2	2	4
Transitional	1	11	18	30
Egalitarian	0	4	2	6
N	1	17	22	40

Twenty-two of the forty parents I interviewed expressed an egalitarian gender ideology, while seventeen others espoused a transitional ideology. It is remarkable that only one of the respondents offered a traditional ideology with respect to aspirations for children, while as many as sixteen identified with a traditional ideology of marital roles. As far as practices are concerned, thirty out of my forty respondents engaged in transitional practices regarding their children. Perhaps as a mark of their middle and upper-middle class composition, the discrepancy between ideology and practice with respect to their aspirations for children is not as glaring as it was for marital roles (see Table 2). My findings on this issue are similar to those of Naidoo and Davis (1988) whose study revealed that South Asian women in Canada have a 'dualistic attitude', one that is 'traditional' with regard to marriage, family and religion, but 'contemporary' on values related to education and careers outside the home.

In order to further understand this 'dualistic' attitude, I examine the connection between the gender ideologies and practices as they appear in the lives of my respondents and their children.

Aspirations for Children's Success

In Rao and Rao's (1984) study among college students in India, it was found that the attitudes of people are gendered as far as children's success was concerned. Men seem to think that parents derive more satisfaction from a son's success than a daughter's and that girls should not be granted as much freedom and independence as boys. Few people in the Indian diaspora in Pittsburgh, however, expressed such views. Parents seemed to derive equal satisfaction from their daughter's as well as their son's successes and spent a great deal of time, money and energy in training their children for a bright future.

This becomes manifest especially in relation to children's education. Since all of them belong to a class of professionals they believe that their children should be given the best opportunities regardless of their gender. Venugopal, a forty-two year old male physician, articulated an egalitarian ideology when he said that he hopes to send both his son and daughter to Ivy League schools for professional education. Even if the girls learn a classical dance like *Bharata Natyam*, they are not expected to make a career of it, rather they are encouraged to become physicians themselves.

However, even though many of my respondents have egalitarian ideologies with regard to children's education, they engage in transitional practices when it comes to their children's career choices. About eighteen of my forty respondents have voiced an egalitarian ideology, but engage in transitional practices. For instance, within the medical profession a number of parents feel strongly that their daughters should keep away from surgery as it would disrupt their family life. My respondents, Shanta and Arun, in separate interviews, said that they discouraged their daughter from going to medical school as it was not necessary for a girl to have a high-pressure career which will affect her 'biological clock' and her family life; as a result, their daughter is now majoring in business management. Shanta felt that a woman's income is secondary and only supplements the man's. She is more worried about the career of her son who she expects will be the primary wage earner for his family. This shows a transitional gender ideology since she has different expectations for her son and her daughter. I say 'transitional' because they do believe that their daughter should have a career but not something as demanding as medicine.

Interestingly, even those respondents who espoused a traditional ideology of marital roles and engaged in traditional practices at home, showed a strong inclination towards an egalitarian or transitional gender ideology with respect to their aspirations for children. One such respondent was Lavanya, who herself grew up in an orthodox brahmin household where it was considered inappropriate for teenage girls to even go out of the house unaccompanied. She said that her desire for education was nipped in the bud by her father who was a conventional patriarch and did not believe in girls' education. She said that although she no longer has an interest in returning to school, she wants her daughter to have a well-rounded education and be given the opportunities that she herself was deprived of.

But, this tendency towards greater egalitarianism with respect to children's education does not manifest itself uniformly in other areas of life, particularly in terms of marriage and dating.

Marriage and Dating

Thirty-one of the forty respondents have children who are teen-agers or younger, but when their children get older they seem to want them to marry within the community, irrespective of whether they have sons or daughters. Many immigrant Indian parents in Pittsburgh have arranged marriages for their children. However, there have been a few cases where young Indian-American women have married white American men of their own choice. Since few of the Indian immigrants in Pittsburgh have children who are of 'marriageable age', I do not have enough data of my own to comment upon their practices in this area.[6]

However, in a study about conflicts and communication gaps between the first and second generation Indian immigrants in Southern California, Priya Agarwal (1991) described the feelings of a young Indian-American woman who is frustrated at the traditional expectations parents have for her because of her gender.

. . . the second generation Indian woman feels that old-world gender roles are still rigidly being upheld for her. . . . 'Throughout my life, society told me I could be whatever I wanted because I was smart and worked hard. Then, suddenly I become of "marriageable age", and I am told I have limits because I am a woman and should marry young. It makes me sick that women are still so defined by men.' (Agarwal 1991:52.)

Many of Agarwal's respondents attributed the gap in gender ideology (particularly with regard to issues of marriage and dating) between parents and children to the fact that for the parental generation, India is a 'pure space' untouched by change. The rapid changes, particularly in urban India are ignored by most im-migrants and they construct an imaginary world where gender ideology is at its patriarchal zenith.

Agarwal (1991) found that Indian parents are more concerned about their girls dating than they are about their sons. Although my respondents expressed a transitional ideology, their practices and strategies are often traditionally gendered in this regard. One of my male respondents, Vaman Rao, said that it was important to have an open relationship with children, especially girls, as they are more vulnerable to the problems of American society.[7]

---

[6] I have not interviewed the children of the immigrant generation for this study to get their side of this complex social issue.

[7] Many Indians believe, like parents in most other cultures, that girls should

However, this discriminatory attitude towards daughters and sons does not seem to surface much in the way parents divide household tasks among their children.

Household Tasks

As far as household chores are concerned, almost all my respondents said that boys and girls have similar chores to do. For example, children, irrespective of their gender, are expected to take care of their own rooms and do other small chores in the house. However, six out of fifteen male respondents pointed out that girls are given more feminine chores like dish-washing, while boys took out garbage and mowed lawns. One of my respondents, Vishnuvardhan, said that he does not differentiate between his boy and girl at this stage as the children were young (thirteen and eleven), but that he can visualize asking his son rather than his daughter to join him in playing tennis or working on his car. His wife, Lavanya, said that she is trying to make her daughter more aware of her femininity by telling her to be soft-spoken and training her to perform domestic religious rituals. These examples reflect the fact that while a majority of my respondents espoused an egalitarian ideology with respect to their children, most of them engaged in transitional practices.

Activities at the Temple

The immigrants' attitudes towards their children could also be seen in the organization of children's activities at the temple as well as in the nature of participation by boys and girls in those activities. There was universal agreement among both male and female respondents about girls having more to do in the temple than boys. As I have shown in chapter III, dance is one of the mechanisms through which Indian tradition is transmitted outside India and it is mostly women and girls who are the transmitters of this tradition. Most of my respondents' daughters are either learning or have learnt *Bharata Natyam* or *Kuchipudi* in the temple.

---

be protected more than boys from the outside world. This is because girls are more vulnerable to the ills of society, such as violence and sexual harassment.

This means that they spend at least two to four hours a week learning classical dance, dressed in traditional Indian attire. The parents feel happy that they are able to provide something 'traditional and Indian' for their girls. The result is that in the process boys are being alienated from the temple.

Respondents who have either occupied key administrative positions at the temple in the past or do so currently have expressed their desire to create something for the boys to do at the temple. In making this distinction, they are assuming that boys and girls need different activities to sustain a commitment and feel an attachment to the institution. The temple recently introduced table tennis to attract the boys on Friday evenings, under the assumption that girls will be kept busy with dance.

Learning classical Indian dance is considered as much a feminine trait as learning ballet in the West. In spite of such feelings in the community and against the initial reservations of his own parents, one boy has been studying *Kuchipudi* at the temple for the past few years. This nonconformity has disturbed the boy's parents, but as his father Vaman Rao said, 'we have learnt to live with it.' This is clearly a case of transitional ideology (because they believe their son and daughter to be equal), but egalitarian practice. Similarly, another woman, Satya, told me that her son wanted to learn dance along with his sister but she and her husband decided that his time was better spent taking tennis lessons. They discouraged him from learning *Bharata Natyam*, she said, but without making him feel that they are doing it because he is a boy. I would classify this kind of behaviour as traditional practice emerging from a transitional ideology.

It is only in the last thirty years in India that classical dance has become almost exclusively a women's art form. Prior to that, girls, especially of the upper castes and classes, were discouraged from performing on stage as it was compared to the *devadasi* system in which the temple dancers were seen also as prostitutes. It was men who dressed up as women and performed in public. However, in post-Independence India, upper-class and caste families began sending their daughters to learn this relatively exclusive and expensive art form. In the last twenty years India's 'high culture' has also been transported to the West mainly by immigrant women and girls. Boys learning classical dance in contemporary times is, thus seen as subverting an important traditional gender practice even though it could be legitimated on the basis that it was an ancient practice.

These varied gender ideologies and practices among the South Indian immigrants should be seen against the cultural backdrop of representations of the 'ideal' Hindu woman and the role of the mass media in fostering and/or reinforcing these cultural representations.

CULTURAL REPRESENTATIONS OF THE 'IDEAL' HINDU WOMAN

The Woman as Pativrata: Mythological Constructs

The Indians in my study were largely socialized into a post-Vedic, patriarchal and patrilocal society in which the woman typically has power only as the mother of a son. The Hindu woman has been characterized in religious, historical as well as mythological texts as either the all-powerful (*Shakti*) or the destructive (*Kali*).[8] People who have been socialized into traditional Hindu culture believe that the woman must either be protected by the male and even worshipped, or else must be controlled. This contradiction can be extended to understand the duality represented by women in Hinduism. On the one hand, women represent nature, and on the other, destruction (Kumari 1990).

The goddess Parvati represents *shakti* or power and energy, the goddess Lakshmi represents wealth and prosperity, and the goddess Saraswati is the one who blesses 'her children' (believers) with knowledge of the arts and education. However, when a goddess like Parvati (represented also as Durga) is angered, she has the power to bring about the destruction of the whole universe. But the power of the male god can be used to soften the destruction.[9]

[8] A note of caution is necessary here about essentializing 'Hindu culture' (see Inden 1990 for a critique of essentialist constructions of Indian society and culture). Hinduism, both as philosophical text as well as a way of life, is extremely complex and varied. It cannot be treated as a monolithic metaphysical text or as a singular document serving as a guide to existence. My account of cultural representations of women in Hinduism is based on a small but influential slice of a multifaceted religion. I engage in a selective reconstruction of popular narratives from Hindu epics which present idealized notions of man and woman.

[9] The concept that women have some dark and dangerous streak which has to be controlled by men is also present in Western culture, where one form of subjugation is violence towards women.

In the process of creation, the woman represents the fertile soil, while the man represents the seed of the future.

During 500 BC–AD 1800 Hindu literature evolved through the *Brahmanas*, the epics (the *Ramayana* and the *Mahabharata*), the *Bhagawad Gita*, the *Manu Dharmasastras*, the *Puranas* and other texts. I will present images of the 'ideal woman' portrayed in the epics and other mythologies. For most Hindus, the ideal woman is personified by Sita, the quintessence of wifely devotion and the heroine of the great epic, *Ramayana*, written by the sage Valmiki. The *Ramayana* is read, listened to, or seen as drama by most Indians even to this day. The legend of Sita, briefly stated, is as follows:

King Janaka of Mithila, while plowing the land one day, found a beautiful baby girl in the earth. He adopted her as his daughter and named her Sita. When she reached marriageable age, he vowed to marry her to the man who could bend a celestial bow. Rama proved to be the only prince who could break the bow into two, after many unsuccessful trials by kings, princes, gods, and demons. Sita was married to Rama and they both proceeded to his father's kingdom of Ayodhya, in keeping with the norm of patrilocal residence.

After a short time, Rama's father banished him to the forest for fourteen years, fulfilling a promise that he had made to his wife Kaikeyi, Rama's step-mother. Sita insisted that, as a virtuous wife, it was her duty to follow Rama, and her decision was met with praise and blessings from her mother and mothers-in-law. In the forest, Sita was abducted by the demon king, Ravana, and forcibly taken to his kingdom. Sita was kidnapped as she literally crossed the forbidden line drawn for her protection. This particular act of Sita is the origin of the now clichéd belief among many Hindus that once a woman crosses the proverbial line, she is vulnerable to attacks that can have disastrous consequences. After months of search, Rama found Sita and rescued her after killing the demon-king Ravana in a long battle. But before re-accepting Sita as his wife, Rama put Sita to a literal test of fire — to prove that she had been untouched and chaste despite months of captivity in another man's home.

Reunited, they returned to the kingdom and were crowned king and queen. However, in his role as the ideal king, Rama succumbed to rumours surrounding his wife's questionable chastity and banished a pregnant Sita to the forest where she gave birth to twin sons a few months later. After the children grew up and returned to their father's kingdom, Sita, not wishing to be put through another ordeal, asked her 'mother', the goddess Earth, to open up and grant her salvation from the travails of human life; subsequently Sita disappeared into the earth. Sudhir Kakar, the well-known Indian psychoanalyst, summarized the roles of Sita and Rama succinctly:

The ideal of womanhood incorporated by Sita is one of chastity, purity, gentle tenderness and a singular faithfulness which cannot be destroyed or even disturbed by her husband's rejection, slights or thoughtlessness . . . Rama may have all the traits of a godlike hero, yet he is also fragile, mistrustful, and jealous, and very much of a conformist, both to his parents' wishes and to social opinion (Kakar 1988:55).

In another popular Hindu myth, Savitri was a woman who insisted on marrying a man knowing full well that he was destined to die within a year. After his death she followed Yama, the god of death, proved her chastity and her devotion to her husband, and tricked Yama first into granting her a wish to beget a hundred sons. She then pleaded for the return of her husband's life as a chaste woman could not have children without her husband. Thus, the ideal of *pativrata*[10] (meaning one who is vowed to her husband) is romanticized through legend and folklore, and reaffirmed through religious ceremonies of various kinds.

Ironically, although Indian society today is far removed from the age of the epics, it nevertheless continues to idealize the character traits of these mythical figures. Identification with Sita contributes to the Hindu woman's adaptation to married life in her husband's extended family and prepares her for her obligatory participation in the family's patriarchal rituals. Many of these ideals seem to be fully incorporated into the lives of most Hindu wives and daughters-in-law. The traditional ideology of marital roles articulated by respondents like Lavanya in my study illustrates the extent to which this ideology has been internalized by women. Others who continued to espouse a traditional ideology as a strategy in spite of transitional practices, did so because of their socialization into a culture in which the woman is expected

[10] The word *pativrata* refers to the individual, while *pativratya* refers to the ideology or the institution of the ideal wife.

to follow the wishes of her husband. There is some empirical evidence to show the prevalence of the *pativratya* ideology among Hindu women in India.

Vanaja Dhruvarajan (1989), in a qualitative study of a small village in southern India, found the ideology of *pativratya* to be widely prevalent among her respondents:

The wife as *pativrata* should be his true helpmate by helping him in every possible way to achieve his goals in life. She should never think that she has an existence apart from her husband. . . . A *pativrata* always eats whatever is left after her husband has eaten. . . . Obeying the command of one's husband without question is a mark of virtue and good conduct . . . He does not have to pay attention even when she is in pain. It does not matter whether he is true to her or not. . . . She believes *Pati pratyaksha devatha* (Husband is the Living God). . . . A true *pativrata* has extraordinary powers which she accumulates by doing austere services to her husband . . . She should listen to stories of great *pativratas* in her spare time so that she is inspired by them (Dhruvarajan 1989:26–7).

Dhruvarajan reports that many of her respondents actually suggested that it might be destructive to give women equal freedom as men. The purity of a woman's body is extremely important, so a man must protect her and she should maintain ritual purity at the cost of her freedom and autonomy.[11] Many of Dhruvarajan's respondents have low self-esteem and a negative self-image.

Dhruvarajan found that women who live in extended families are more likely to follow the ideology of *pativratya* with great deference than those who are part of a nuclear family. To be a good wife signifies being a good woman. Day-to-day behaviour is structured through certain deferential customs, and women are constantly reminded of their subordinate position in society. Dhruvarajan also found that the Hindu epics and mythologies continue to provide models of the ideal woman, reinforcing the ideology of *pativratya*. These values are transmitted from one generation to the other, not only informally at home, but also through folk culture, including village concerts and drama, and the mass media.

---

[11] Ritual purity for a traditional Hindu woman involves among other things maintaining physical distance from others during her menstrual periods. She is supposed to mingle with people only after she has 'purified' herself with a ritual bath on the fourth day of her period.

Reinforcing Traditional Roles: Media Images

In recent times, the most popular shows on Indian television have been serialized episodes from the Hindu epics. In 1988, the *Ramayana* was telecast every Sunday morning and millions of people stayed glued to their sets and empathized with the trials and tribulations of many of its central characters. Sita's image as the *pativrata* was once again resurrected as a character with whom women ought to identify. In 1989, after the *Ramayana* completed its run, the other major epic, *Mahabharata*, took over television drama and enjoyed even greater popularity.

Popular culture in India is replete with notions of ideal womanhood and especially now, at a time when the country is witnessing the rise of a Hindu fundamentalist movement, images of women like Sita and Savitri have become a part of everyday discourse. When asked what her concept of a liberated Indian woman was, one of the spokespersons of the Bharatiya Janata Party, the right-wing Hindu fundamentalist party, said: 'She is a combination of Sita and Savitri. We need to fight against the atrocities committed on women, but fight without rebelling or upsetting the family' (Menon 1993:16). Many Indian feminists are now concerned that the resurgence of fundamentalism might well mean the further perpetuation of patriarchal practices.

The power of the media to create, select and convey particular kinds of images about women cannot be underestimated. Participants at India's first National Women's Studies Conference held in 1981 blamed the media for promoting stereotypes of women. The traditional roles of the subservient female and the dominant male are repeatedly reinforced on the Indian screen. A woman is considered to be a goddess by society because of her readiness to sacrifice for her family members (Hegde and Dasgupta 1984). Indian movies represent the ideal woman as one who revels in suffering and sacrifice. An analysis of the mistreatment of women in society as portrayed in films shows that films follow the existing male dominant ideology (Dasgupta and Hegde 1988). According to the authors, such portrayals reaffirm the patriarchal order and perpetuate the existing dichotomy of sex roles.

Even movies and television shows which claim to portray progressive women asserting their individuality rarely help promote positive attitudes about women. Rebellious female characters are shown to eventually succumb to dominant patriarchal ideologies, and those who overcome them are shown to be doing it at some cost (Dasgupta and Hegde 1988). Women are portrayed as facing a large number of insurmountable obstacles and by the time a divorced woman pulls her life back together she undergoes traumatic experiences. Film and television, because of their easy accessibility, reach out both to the educated as well as the illiterate, and to urban as well as rural people. Whether the images presented in the media are apparently 'progressive' or blatantly regressive, they seem to contribute to the reinforcement of patriarchal values among people in various sections of society.

Most of the first-generation Indian immigrants in my study grew up in India amidst these images of women and gender roles. Moreover, with the global technological revolution in the 1990s, popular culture in India is quite easily transmitted to immigrants in other parts of the world. The villagers in Dhruvarajan's study, the urbanites in India, and the Indian immigrants in the United States or the Middle-East all watch the same shows and films through videos and on ethnic television. Appadurai (1990) calls this kind of electronic transmission of images across the world, 'mediascapes.'

What is most important about these mediascapes is that they provide . . . large and complex repertoires of images, narratives and ethnoscapes to viewers throughout the world. . . . The lines between the realistic and the fictional landscapes they see are blurred, so that the further away these audiences are from the direct experiences of metropolitan life, the more likely are they to construct imagined worlds which are chimerical, aesthetic, even fantastic objects . . . (Appadurai 1990:9).

The 'imagined' world for immigrants is India with all its legends and folktales; and often the patriarchal images in the media appear to be quite real for those who watch and internalize them. Children born in the United States are also exposed to this mythical world through the media, influencing their socialization.

It is not surprising, therefore, that I found a majority of my respondents (both male and female) espousing a traditional ideology of marital roles. One such respondent, Malathi, has a large video collection of all the mythological films which her family watches regularly. When children are socialized through the attractive medium of videos and television about Sita and Savitri, they might internalize the patriarchal ideologies embedded in such narratives.

The view that traditional Hindu ideals of womanhood may have negative influences is challenged by some scholars who assert that the idea of women as weak and inferior was in fact inherited from the West (Liddle and Joshi 1986). According to this perspective, the status of Indian women was traditionally quite high and it was Western imperialism that magnified the image of the oppressed Indian woman. In my study, a male scientist, forty-five year old Rajaraman, speaks about egalitarian gender ideology in Hindu philosophy and the actual patriarchal practice:

If you understand our scriptures and literature correctly, the place of women in India is so wonderful, although it is not practiced. Sita, Draupadi . . . and all great women saints were held in great esteem. Maybe it is Western influence, but the general impression given is that India is a macho country and that women don't have much freedom and all that. But I don't think that women are greatly mistreated. If you worship goddesses and you see their form in all women, how can you mistreat them?

Even as this respondent speaks of gender equality, he is reinforcing the image of the ideal woman as pure and saintly which, far from being egalitarian, can be a terrible burden. This assumption that Hinduism accords women a highly respected position has been promoted by nationalist historians in India (Poonacha 1993:438). This is only another facet of patriarchy that is couched within the construction of the woman as goddess. Moreover, not all my respondents subscribe to the thesis that there was greater equality in India, especially those who lived in an extended family under the supervisory role of the mother-in-law.

However, the cultural constructions of the 'ideal' Hindu woman and their propagation through the mass media cannot entirely account for the variations in gender ideologies and practices among the immigrants in this study. Contemporary social changes in India, literacy and education and their urban backgrounds in India should also be considered to explain tendencies towards more transitional and egalitarian practices.

Education and Social Change in India

Gender ideologies of immigrants in the United States can thus be compared and contrasted with the gender ideologies and strategies of urban, educated women and men in India. Most of the Indian immigrants to the United States were educated in urban or semi-urban India and either pursue higher education or work as professionals in the US. Shamita Das Dasgupta's (1986) study about sex roles of Asian Indian women in the United States revealed that the most important factor in determining non-traditional gender roles might be the number of years an individual has gone to school in the United States. She says that it is not just the length of stay in the United States, but participation in the Western education system that generates egalitarian thinking among the Asian Indian women in her study (Dasgupta 1986:309).

Fewer than half (fifteen out of forty) of my respondents went to school in the US, but the backgrounds of some of the others suggest that Dasgupta's findings could be extended to include the influences of liberal education in India. One of my respondents, Ramani, who is in her early forties and works in a hospital, was raised and educated in a major metropolitan city in India (in a Westernized school system). Her egalitarian gender ideology or practices, she asserted, are no different now than they were when she was in India. She said she and her siblings were raised with an emphasis on good education and that there was no strict gendered division of labour at home. Ramani and her forty-five year old husband Suresh share the work at home as do many other dual-career couples in my study. Suresh attributed their egalitarian lifestyle to the fact that he is from Kerala, a southern Indian state not only with a history of matrilineal societies but also has the highest literacy rates in the country for both men and women. He explained:

It is the woman who plays an important role in the family. Seventy-five years ago, there were certain families in which women had their B.A. degrees. Why? Because the woman in that house had decided that her daughter will do her B.A. This still holds good to this day.

But this egalitarianism is certainly not representative of the attitudes and practices of all educated Indians.

An examination of the context in which people of my respondents' social class (and mine) were educated in India, especially women, gives us a sense of why there is no necessary correlation between education and egalitarianism. Rama Mehta (1970), in her study of Western-educated Hindu women in India, sought to understand the influence of education over their traditional value system. A majority of the fifty women she interviewed said that their parents sent them to college to bide time till marriage rather than to acquire proficiency in a particular discipline. Education was not a way to attain economic independence, as working outside the home was against the norms established by the cult of domesticity. These women's mothers, who were themselves not formally educated, realized the need for their daughters to be educated just enough to make them 'eligible brides' but they did not encourage unmarried women to work. Once married, many of these women said, their husbands were proud to have educated wives, but did not want them to work outside the home, as it was necessary for them to be home with their children.

Another study of Indian college students' attitudes to sex roles arrived at similar conclusions (Rao and Rao 1984). This study examined the relationship between social changes such as urbanization and industrialization and sex role attitudes in India. Both men and women thought that a woman's most important task is caring for her children and husband, and that if her working outside the home is inconvenient to other family members, she should give up her job.

The above studies suggest that the cultural representations of the Hindu woman are not merely the substance of past myths and mythologies, but have become a part of the contemporary Indian social milieu, one from which most of the immigrants in my study have originated. An example from my study of someone who expressed a traditional gender ideology is Venugopal, who went to medical school in urban India in the 1970s. His rationale for marrying a homemaker was as follows:

I married a homemaker only for two reasons. If two people are working, you don't need a marriage. In my case, I don't have to make her work. That is an advantage she has. The second thing is I wanted somebody to be more attentive to my kids. She is very dedicated to the kids. One-third of her time is completely for the kids. She runs around and does a lot for the kids. . . . I look at her lifestyle and I think that she got more than she bargained for.

Venugopal, like the respondents in the Raos' study, believes that women are better off if they give primacy to the family and the husband over their own personal ambitions. He believes that marriage is the most crucial and important phase in a woman's life, and all other pursuits — intellectual, educational or political

— are merely means for attaining the most suitable husband. Although Venugopal has these expectations for his wife and rationalizes any 'rebellion' on her part as the price of Americanization, he is prepared to send his daughter as well as his son to an Ivy League school. Thus in terms of his children's education his aspirations may appear to be egalitarian, but I would wait until his ten year old daughter grows up before writing the last word on it.

CONCLUSION

In this chapter, I have examined the gender ideologies among the immigrants in my study and compared them with their practices. There are gaps in ideology and practice that can be explained in terms of a gender strategy. It is often strategically convenient for women to pursue egalitarian practices, but voice a transitional ideology. A number of female as well as male respondents espoused a traditional or transitional ideology while they were engaged in egalitarian practices. It gives men the satisfaction of being in control and makes the women feel empowered at the same time.

In addition to the discrepancy between ideology and practice, I also found that the immigrants in my study tended toward a particular gender ideology with respect to their own marital roles and quite another with respect to their aspirations for their children. I have suggested that the roots of the traditional gender ideology espoused by many of my respondents lie in cultural values embedded in ancient myths and folklore and transmitted by media images. However, as many of my respondents also tended to follow transitional or egalitarian practices, I have sought to explain the variations through more contemporary social changes in India. These social changes and their influences on my respondents, along with the effects of immigration, could also explain the nature of participation and leadership roles of South Indian women at the S.V. temple (see chapter IV).

It is also necessary for me to compare here the gendered behaviour patterns at their homes with those in the temple. As I have discussed above, many of the immigrant men share in the domestic tasks even if they have a traditional gender ideology. In the temple also there is a shared division of labour and men and women participate together in administrative as well as ritual-related tasks. However, some degree of gendered division of labour persists in the temple kitchen as well as in traditionally feminine chores such as making garlands. With regard to the activities of the children, I have shown earlier in this chapter that their activities tend to be quite gendered at the temple. Where there are boys learning classical dance, it is still considered an embarrassment. Even while the Indian-American children are enacting traditional ideologies, their participation is quite superficial and their socialization into patriarchal Indian culture is not intense. This is hardly surprising because their mothers themselves feel they are far more liberated than they would have been in India and encourage achievement and success in both their female and male children.

For many of my women respondents, life in the US after immigration has been to some extent a liberating experience. They are able to exercise a degree of autonomy to do certain things that would have been difficult had they been living in India. For some others, however, life in the US has only been a continuation of their urban experiences in India.

VI

Conclusion:
Gender in the Making of
an Immigrant Community

In this study, I have examined the ways in which a particular deterritorialized group — the South Indian immigrants in Pittsburgh — has creatively reconstructed its identity in an attempt to overcome feelings of generalized homelessness. A visible outcome of this process of reconstruction was the birth of a temple, a symbolic world constituting nostalgia for remembered places. The efforts of this immigrant group to build a community, centred around a religious institution, cannot be described as a simple, unproblematic process of transplantation of old values, norms, and roles in a new context. The renegotiation of gender relations in the community is a significant aspect of the epistemological ruptures that accompanied the complex process of immigration. Traditional gender roles and relations have been perpetuated in some cultural practices, but transformed in others, often resulting in greater egalitarianism.

The tendency among the immigrants towards what I characterize as egalitarianism must be understood within a cultural context that is specific to their situation. I am convinced that a number of South Indian women in Pittsburgh experience greater freedom compared to their lives back home or with the lives of their mothers. These women are educated, economically secure, fairly autonomous in decision-making, religious, and family-oriented. They not only confound the 'Third World' stereotype constructed by some western feminists, but they are also participants in transforming certain patriarchal practices in their families and communities.[1] The lived experiences of these women and the level of gender consciousness among them may not appear to be adequately feminist (as the term is understood in the West). But I contend that rather than applying gender as a universal construct, women's experiences must be understood in terms of the concrete historical and political practices within which they are embedded. The assumption that women are a coherent group with a homogeneity of interests, problems and desires, regardless of differences in class, ethnic and racial origins, or religion, implies the notion that gender as a category can be applied universally.[2]

Recently, some feminists have been calling for greater specificity in studies of gender and emphasizing that gender is a multifaceted category open to change and variation (Ginsburg and Tsing 1990; Harding 1990). Anna Lowenhaupt Tsing (1993:18) suggests that particular forms of 'female marginality' must be examined 'in relation to the conditions of women's lives — as immigrants, minorities, wealthy, poor, black, white, sex workers, maids, or academics. As I have explained in chapter II, my work borrows from both postmodern feminism and standpoint feminism. With the postmodern feminists I believe in contextualizing the women's experiences rather than speaking of universal sisterhood and with the standpoint feminists I believe that it is necessary to understand women's problems from their own perspective.

Donna Gabaccia's caution against dismissing women's identification with their families as 'false consciousness' is relevant in analysing the experiences of groups such as the South Indians in Pittsburgh. The women in my study have carried with them certain cultural values and make conscious choices to lead their lives within particular ideological and social contexts. Valuable insights could be gained about these immigrant women and their ideologies and practices by locating them within their own cultural

[1] In a valuable critique of feminist scholarship, Chandra Mohanty points out that much of western feminist writings construct the 'Third World' woman as 'ignorant, poor, uneducated, tradition-bound, religious, domesticated, family-oriented, victimized, etc.' (Mohanty 1988:65). The Western woman, on the other hand, is represented as educated, modern and having the freedom to make her own decisions. Mohanty emphasizes the need to move away from such monolithic analytic constructs.

[2] This notion of universality is expressed, for example, in book titles such as *Sisterhood is Global* (Morgan 1984).

context. For instance, all Islamic women in *purdah* cannot be seen as a homogeneously oppressed group (Minces 1980). Recent works on Islam and gender (Zuhur 1992) point out that the veil is now being worn by some Islamic feminists as a means to subvert the very patriarchal values that it originally imposed. We cannot ignore the agency that these women experience in making decisions about the actual use of the veil or the *purdah*. Thus, these Islamic women or the women in my study cannot be characterized simply as oppressed women and neither can they be accused of lacking a feminist consciousness.

I emphasize that women whose primary identification is with their families are not necessarily oppressed women who need to be rescued from the clutches of patriarchy. The women in my study are definitely instrumental in perpetuating certain patriarchal practices but they are also able to find some form of liberation or empowerment in their diasporic situation. In that sense, my study could be seen as a specific instance of understanding women's ideologies and practices from their own standpoints. How do they experience empowerment in a conventional patriarchal religious institution? I argue that they are in the process of feminizing the religious institution and negotiating new gender roles for themselves. Many of them have already experienced egalitarianism in their workplaces and to a great extent in their homes.

In my analysis of immigrant experiences, I have combined the 'woman-centred' and 'gender-integrated' approaches discussed by Gerda Lerner (1979), focusing on women whose voices have been largely muffled under gender-blind (or even male-centred) surveys of immigrant lives. The feminist ethnography I have attempted here showed that far from being passive followers or victims of their male kin, the South Indian women in Pittsburgh played a significant role in establishing the temple and actively engaged in tasks that seek to sustain it. In fact, by making their private goals of socialization of children and cultural reproduction the central aspect of the public religious institution's agenda, these women have not only feminized the public sphere, but are also involved in a renegotiation of the public/private dichotomy.

Religious institutions in many ways can be seen as mediating between the public and private spheres. The S.V. temple in Pittsburgh is one such institution which displays features of both the spheres. By substituting as a 'second home' in the celebration of festivals and other cultural events, the temple and the community which uses that space serve as a surrogate extended family. Women play a leading role in creating and maintaining fictive kinship networks among members of the community. These private relationships among the women often become the basis on which the community carries out many of its public activities.

The temple, as a formal organization, also exhibits many characteristics of the public sphere. A Hindu temple is itself a traditional organization that prescribes certain rigid roles and rituals for women and men to perform. With considerable revenues to manage, the temple is administered through a hierarchy of boards and committees, a majority of whose members are elected. Instead of being confined to the traditionally-defined domestic sphere, women have assumed leadership positions in the temple's administrative structure from the inception of the temple. By performing ably in such rational bureaucratic roles, the women have succeeded in infusing the public institution with their more private aspirations, thereby feminizing it.

These private aspirations are realized through attempts to create a cultural heritage with which their children will be able to identify. As part of this process of cultural reproduction, the Indian immigrants both accommodate and resist influences from the dominant, host culture. Gender identity is an important dimension of both the first generation's efforts at cultural reproduction as well as the socialization of the second generation. In certain activities at the temple, traditional gender divisions are replicated, but the meanings of those conventions have been subverted and redefined. For instance, even as some kind of segregated spaces are maintained for women and men, women seem to derive a sense of belonging and power through their activities in exclusively female spaces.

The women in my study are not feminists who consciously fight to emphasize the female power symbolized by Hindu goddesses and nor do they seek to rewrite Hindu myths from the standpoint of the female goddesses.[3] They embrace traditional

---

[3] A large number of feminist studies in sociology of religion concentrate on the efforts of some scholars to rewrite religious texts and reinterpret theological scriptures from a feminist perspective. There are few studies that seek to reinterpret Hindu religious texts and a discussion of this nature is beyond the purview of the present study.

gender ideologies of marital roles while professing egalitarian ideologies regarding other aspects such as education and careers of their children. In practice, even some of the women with traditional ideologies live in households where housework and childcare is shared by both spouses. They also enjoy a certain autonomy in decision-making about children's socialization, family finances, and the extent of the family's participation in the community.

There is, thus, a disjunction between some of the gender ideologies and actual practices of the women and men I interviewed. Some of these incongruities can be explained on the basis of their social backgrounds in India. Indians in urban areas are usually socialized into having a traditional gender ideology with regard to marriage and family, but an egalitarian one regarding education and careers of women (Liddle and Joshi 1986). The immigrants carry these ideologies with them to the US where the spirit of achievement in one's career becomes especially focused (Naidoo and Davis 1988). It is the influence of the host society to some extent, along with the middle-class values in India that shape the education and career choices of immigrants. Similarly, it is the culturally pluralist ideology of the immigrant society that encourages them to reassert and underline the importance of their traditional background.

As a feminist researcher, it was not difficult to understand the range of ideologies that the immigrants carried with them from urban India, because I myself am an Indian woman with an urban, educated, upper-caste, middle-class background. In that sense, I was an insider to the community and had the advantage of knowing and being able to take for granted certain aspects of the immigrants' values and behaviour. However, there were other considerations such as my transitional situation as a student and my not being a parent that gave me an outsider status in the community. While as an insider I could share some of their experiences, as an outsider I strove to observe how the experiences of the women in my study were different from mine. My research in the Indian diaspora in Pittsburgh left a lasting impact on my own interaction with the Indian immigrants. After three years of research I have come to empathize much more with the community's central concerns and dilemmas. I have presented the lives of the women and men in the community as I have observed and heard.

I have not been an 'objective and detached' researcher in the positivist sense as I have interacted and shared my own experiences with my respondents for nearly three years. For instance, prior to conducting my research, I would write off gender segregation in parties and at the temple as reaffirming patriarchy. It was only after I immersed myself in the field that I came to realize the empowering potential of these gendered spaces. Women wanted to be away from their husbands and interact with friends for an extended period of time.

Case studies like mine reveal not only the specific concerns of the women and men in the community I studied, but also bring to light aspects of social and cultural life that could be explored in further research on other immigrant groups. I believe that case studies of women's experiences enhance our ability to examine women's lives in cross-cultural or comparative contexts (Reinharz 1992:166). Further, the ethnographic case study I have conducted helped me to rectify, to some extent, the 'gynopia' (Reinharz 1992), or the inability to perceive the existence of women, in studies of immigrant communities. The importance of ethnographic research to study immigrant religious institutions, in particular, has been underlined by Kivisto (1992). For him, such case studies help in 'tracing and explicating facets of the internal' dynamics of institutional religion and the salience of religious belief in the various immigrant communities' (Kivisto 1992:104).

REFLECTIONS ON THE FUTURE OF INDIAN IMMIGRANTS

The Indian diaspora in the United States is now fairly well-established, having accomplished many of its members' economic and cultural goals. It is likely that the community will gradually shift its energies and resources to other areas of life. In 1991, the Indian Ambassador to the US appealed to the Indian immigrants to invest in the promotion of India Studies in American institutions of higher education instead of continuing to build more religious institutions. Partly because of the Ambassador's initiative, there are now Chairs in India Studies at the University of California, Berkeley and Columbia University, New York. India Studies has been established as part of the University Centre for International Studies at the University of Pittsburgh. There are also steps to start a Centre for the Study of Indian Classical Music and Dance.

As a step in this direction, the Indians in Pittsburgh started raising funds for endowing an Indian Nationality Room at the University's Cathedral of Learning. Indian women in Pittsburgh continue to play a prominent role in some of these activities.

As the community in Pittsburgh grows along with the Asian Indians in other parts of the diaspora, their approaches to emerging problems will yield topics for further research. For example, in major metropolitan areas such as New York and New Jersey, where there are sizeable numbers of Indian immigrants, women's organizations are dealing with issues such as domestic violence and 'green card divorces'.[4] These women's groups are quite distinct from the larger community that centres around cultural and religious activities and sometimes come into conflict with the latter's goals (Bhattacharjee 1992). An area that is of significant interest in the study of the Indian diaspora is that of gender and law. In the Indian diaspora in Canada, some cases have come to light recently where the law was indifferent to instances of domestic violence in the Indian community because it was considered 'acceptable' in Indian culture. Research into such legal discrimination might help victimized women obtain sound legal aid. Although I have argued against the trend toward victimologies in feminist research for fear of portraying women only as victims, it is no doubt important to understand different aspects of women's concerns in the Indian diaspora and highlight the pathologies of institutionalized patriarchy.

Patricia Caplan (1985), in her study of privileged women in India, says that upper-class women's organizations are instrumental in reproducing class structure as well as patriarchal norms and values. Although the S.V. temple is not a women's organization, women's participation in the organizational structure of the temple could be compared to women's participation in certain groups in India. The women and men who frequent the Pittsburgh temple are quite conscious of their class position and attempt to reproduce those aspects of religion and culture that have been traditionally associated with wealth and power. So, unlike some of the women in New York, the Pittsburgh Indian women have not created more progressive women's groups that

---

[4] There are several instances of Indian men marrying Indian women who are permanent residents or citizens of the US and later abandoning them after they receive their green cards (Ramaseshan 1992).

deal with problems such as domestic violence and sexual harassment. But, as the number of Indian women in universities in Pittsburgh increases, it is likely that women's activist groups will be formed. It remains to be seen whether the emergence of such groups will lead to new alliances among the older and newer immigrant women and to the formation of a more explicit feminist consciousness among them such as in Chicago.

However, as I have maintained in this study, the absence of a feminist consciousness does not necessarily mean that the immigrant women in Pittsburgh lead a subdued and passive life. Although many of the women in my study came to the US as 'dependent migrants', they now feel socially and economically secure enough to actively encourage and sponsor the migration of their family members in India. These women tend to promote the immigration of their kin because they find the experience of immigration much more positive than do men, as it allowed women to break with traditional roles (Foner 1978; Pessar 1984). It is possible that a decade from now, most of the immigrants will have primary kin in the country and one might see a weakening of surrogate family ties within the community.

The second generation Indian-Americans will most likely continue to be a major cause for concern for their parents. As their children are growing up, the immigrants in my study increasingly worry that they might not marry within the community. Many of the immigrants' children are still in their early teens, so the concern about dating and marriage has not yet become central. But as the children of some of the older immigrants in the community have married non-Indians, the issue is gradually creeping into the community's agenda. Some parents feel that the temple as a setting for social interaction is restrictive for the young Indian-Americans and many of them would not want to return to it once they are out of the home. The building of a community centre where Indian-American teenagers are allowed freedom to interact without the restrictive presence of parents has been suggested by some members of the community. It is possible that in the foreseeable future there will be more opportunities for Indian-American teenagers to date and mix among themselves, and the same parents who were engaged in building a religious institution might raise funds to create social centres beyond the temple.

The future role of the second generation in maintaining the

ethnic distinctiveness of the Indian diasporic community will be interesting to follow. On college campuses all over the US, there are Indian-Americans who are rethinking their heritage from their own perspectives and free from parental direction. Among other things, they meet regularly through organizations of Indian-American students on campuses, enroll in classes on Indian culture and religion, and go on study programmes to India. At a time when Hindu fundamentalism is on the rise in India, the diasporic Indian and, particularly, the second generation immigrant is caught in the middle of the conflicts between the more secular and the sectarian movements. Many of the young Indian-Americans are recruited by the *Vishwa Hindu Parishad* (VHP) in their efforts to promote Hindu fundamentalism in the United States.[5] In August 1993 the VHP organized a massive conference in Washington, D.C. under the title of 'World Vision 2000' where for the first time the organization openly engaged the second generation Indians in their efforts to politicize Hinduism (*Sanskriti*, 1993).

As this fundamentalist movement becomes more firmly entrenched in the US and as Indian-Americans get more deeply implicated in the tensions between the fundamentalist and the secular groups, one might see the redefinition of Hinduism in the US. Raymond Williams suggests that this reconstruction of the meaning of 'Hindu' will be accompanied by a broader 'redefinition of boundaries through the manipulation of symbols and the expansion of their cultural contextualization so as to include as many Asian Indians as possible under a single religious identity' (Williams 1988:54). The NRIs also play quite an active role in contributing funds to political groups in India. Many Sikh immigrants to England and Canada have promoted the Khalistan movement and it might be a harsh fact that the Hindutva movement in India is being promoted by Hindus abroad. The role of women in this new movement would be interesting to study particularly since conventional gender roles continue to operate in the new scenario.

As I have explained in chapter I, the global Indian diaspora has made a significant impact in the political arena apart from their contributions to the cultural and religious spheres. In the

[5] The *Vishwa Hindu Parishad* is one of the most widespread Hindu fundamentalist organizations in the world today. A substantial part of their resources come from immigrant Hindu groups all over the world.

Caribbean, people of Indian origin have made a significant contribution and have assumed prominent political positions. Thomas Abraham, the President of the New York-based Global Organization for People of Indian Origin asserts that they will be a powerful economic force in the future (Khan 1996). The Non-Resident Indians in USA and Europe have made significant educational and scientific contributions and are now involved in large-scale business corporations. A number of Indians figure in Britain's list of the one hundred richest people, notable among whom are the businessmen G.P. Hinduja and Swraj Paul. Although the NRIs seem to be a formidable economic force in various parts of the diaspora, they have not made any notable contribution to the Indian economy. Their contributions to the Indian economy will be dependent to a large extent on the direction given to the present economic policies by the newly-formed government in 1996.

SOME DIRECTIONS FOR FURTHER RESEARCH

With the coming-of-age of the second generation Indian-Americans, the anxieties of the immigrant community regarding cultural reproduction and retention of cultural identity have been exacerbated. One of the most important reasons for ethnic congregations to emerge and flourish in a culturally plural society is the desire to transmit religious and cultural values to the American-born children. In a proposal for a large ethnographic project on New Ethnic and Immigrant Congregations in the US, Warner (1993b) stresses the importance of understanding emerging religious congregations in an increasingly pluralistic society such as the United States. The S.V. temple in Pittsburgh and the South Indians who frequent it, constitute one such congregation. Case studies of such communities will help illuminate macro-level issues in the contemporary United States such as increasing racial and ethnic diversity, the expansion of the religious economy, and multicultural curriculum in schools. My study also contributes to the emerging research on Asian Indians in the United States in general and, more specifically, on Asian Indian women. By focusing on gender dynamics among a section of the Asian Indians in Pittsburgh, I hope to have drawn attention to the differential effects of immigration on women and men.

All my respondents mentioned the need to explain to their children their Indian and Hindu identity. Their concerns reflect the general cultural predicament of new ethnic and immigrant groups in the United States. These dilemmas among immigrant communities have now assumed a truly inter-generational character as the second generation challenges the first generation's notions of identity, resists the latter's attempt to impart cultural education, and sometimes rebels against the mandate to conform (Agarwal 1991). Of course, this is not to deny that there are many second generation Indian-Americans who have quietly accepted the mandate and some who have enthusiastically embraced the Indian and/or Hindu identity transmitted to them by their parents. Some Indian-American women, after they got married, became an integral part of the Indian community in Pittsburgh.

It would be interesting to study the effects of religious socialization on the second generation Indian-Americans. I observed and interacted with some of these Indian-Americans during my research at the Pittsburgh temple. They expressed an interest in interacting with someone who was much younger than their parents but, like the latter, grew up in India.[6] While some among them continue to give classical dance performances into their late teens and early twenties and express their desires to visit India, there are others who want to have nothing to do with the temple or with the Indian community once they reach adulthood. There is an acceptance of their 'Indianess' among those who continue to frequent the temple. Some of these children enjoy voluntary work at the temple because it makes them feel important and gives them an opportunity to hang out with others of their age.

I learned in my meetings with the second generation Indians that these young people who were born and brought up in the US have their own strong values and opinions which often did not coincide with those of their parents. On the one hand, they resist their parents' efforts to mould them into accepting the identity of a 'good Hindu' or Indian and, on the other, they struggle to counter the stereotypes about their generation captured in the derogatory label

[6] In social gatherings among Indian students, I often found myself defending this generation against unfair criticism and cruel jokes. I felt that in situations such as these, the role of an ethnographer ought to be more than merely collecting data. One has to understand the diversities among the people we are interviewing and observing and be sensitive to their dilemmas and feelings.

of ABCDs (American Born Confused *Desi*) and in the innumerable jokes that abound about their particular situation.[7]

The increase in communication ties between India and the US has led to a proliferation of cultural exchanges between the two countries. As a result, one encounters cultural ironies such as the conscious attempt to Indianize children born in the US, while back in India teenagers grow up on a constant diet of Western cultural artifacts such as MTV, Pepsi, and Reeboks. In my study, I have focused on a single group's efforts to recreate an 'imagined community' for themselves and their children. In my future work, I propose to focus on the varied responses of second generation Indian immigrants to the socialization that they have experienced. I would like to understand how the second generation deals with problems of identity and their cultural distinctiveness within the US.

With the exception of a few self-reflective accounts by second generation immigrants themselves (Agarwal 1991), a systematic social science effort in understanding the second generation perspectives of immigrant culture is yet to emerge. I would like to probe further into the ways in which the second generation Indian-Americans in Pittsburgh have responded to the temple in particular and, more generally, to their parents' attempts at inculcating in them an Indian identity.

The Indian diaspora is now a significant group among the new immigrants in the US. I think there are several issues besides inter-generational conflict and tensions that could be examined in other social scientific analyses. Comparative studies among different Indian congregations (e.g. Hindu temples and Sikh gurdwaras or Islamic centres) would help in understanding the various ways in which men and women from the same country, but of different religious persuasions, deal with issues of identity, gender, and conflict. Apart from the two Hindu temples, the Pittsburgh area also has a South Asian Islamic centre and a Sikh gurdwara. A larger comparative study would aid in understanding the nature of religious pluralism among the Indians in Pittsburgh and elsewhere.

[7] The word *desi* is best translated as 'indigene or native'. The label mocks at the complexities of this generation's multiple identities as American, Indian, and Indian-American. The label itself is a creation of visiting students from India: a group that has little understanding about the second generation's cultural dilemmas.

Indian immigrants are varied, not only in terms of religion, but also by region, language, caste, and class. For example, the Hindus in Pittsburgh itself have split into two separate congregations along regional lines. A comparative analysis of the Hindu-Jain temple and the S.V. temple in Pittsburgh would help understand whether gender dynamics are similar in both institutions or are uniquely different. Although I have not yet conducted such a comparative analysis, an informal appraisal of the newsletter of the Hindu-Jain temple makes it apparent that women do not play as central a role in the administration as they do in the S.V. temple. I would like to understand the reasons for these differences and also reflect upon some of the similarities between the two groups.

Research on the Indian immigrants' participation in the American economy would be another interesting arena for social scientific inquiry, because most of the post-1965 immigrants have been educated, middle-class professionals. The medical profession is particularly significant as there are a number of male and female Indian immigrant physicians and surgeons in the United States hospitals. A comparative study of gender dynamics among these doctors with those among male and female doctors in urban India would possibly throw light on the impact of immigration on the people in this profession.

For the past three decades, the Indian immigrants have been assimilating into the American economy while struggling to remain culturally distinctive. They have emerged as one of the more economically successful middle-class groups and use that success to participate actively in establishing religious institutions in the US. The flourishing of Hindu temples in the United States and elsewhere in the Indian diaspora is obviously an indication of the conscious attempts being made to preserve religion. But, more importantly, for the women who become bearers of religious traditions in the diaspora, it involves a complex process of negotiating with their ethnic, class, and gender identities. It is through this negotiation of identities that the Indian immigrant women play an active role in reconstructing community in the diaspora.

Bibliography

Acker, Joan, Kate Barry and Johanna Esseveld (1983), 'Objectivity and Truth: Problems in Doing Feminist Research', in *Women's Studies Forum*, 6(4), pp. 423–35.

Agarwal, Priya (1991), *Passage from India: Post 1965 Indian Immigrants and their Children* (Paolo Verdes, CA: Yuvati Publications).

Albrecht, Stan L. and Marie Cornwall (1989), 'Life Events and Religious Change', *Review of Religious Research*, 31, 1 (September), pp. 23–38.

Anderson, Benedict (1983), *Imagined Communities: Reflections on the Origin and Spread of Nationalism* (London: Verso).

Andezian, Sossie (1986), 'Women's Roles in Organizing Symbolic Life: Algerian Female Immigrants in France', in *International Migration: The Female Experience*, Rita James Simon and Caroline B. Brettell (eds.) (New Jersey: Rowman & Allanheld), pp. 254–65.

Anwar, Muhammad (1979), *The Myth of Return: Pakistanis in Britain* (London: Heinemann).

Appadurai, Arjun (1981), *Worship and Conflict under Colonial Rule: A South Indian Case Study* (Cambridge: Cambridge University Press).

—— (1988), 'Putting Hierarchy in its Place', *Cultural Anthropology*, 3, 1, pp. 36–49.

—— (1990), 'Disjuncture and Difference in the Global Cultural Economy', *Public Culture*, 2, 2 (Spring), pp. 1–24.

—— (1993), 'Patriotism and its Futures', *Public Culture*, 5, pp. 411–29.

Armstrong, John A. (1982), *Nation and Nationalism* (Chapel Hill: The University of North Carolina Press).

Arnopoulos, Sheila McLeod (1979), *Problems of Immigrant Women in the Canadian Labor Force* (Ottawa: Canadian Advisory Council on the Status of Women).

Baker, Patricia (1987), 'Doing Fieldwork in a Canadian Bank: Issues of Gender and Power', *Resources for Feminist Research*, 16, pp. 45–7.

Barth, Fredrick (1969), *Ethnic Groups and Boundaries* (Boston: Little Brown).

Bell, Diane (1983), *Daughters of the Dreaming* (North Sydney: George Allen & Unwin).

Bellah, Robert N. et al. (1985), *Habits of the Heart: Individualism and Commitment in American Life* (New York: Harper and Row).

Benhabib, Seyla (1992), *Situating the Self: Gender, Community and Postmodernism in Contemporary Ethics* (Polity Press).

Benhabib, Seyla and Drucilla Cornell (eds.) (1987), *Feminism as Critique: On the Politics of Gender* (Minneapolis: University of Minnesota Press).

Berk, Sarah Fernstermaker (1985), *The Gender Factory: The Apportionment of Work in American Households* (New York: Plenum Press).

Berry, J.W. (1988), 'Acculturation and Psychological Adaptation: A Conceptual Overview', in *Ethnic Psychology: Research and Practice with Immigrants, Refugees, Native Peoples, Ethnic Groups, and Sojourners*, J.W. Berry and R.C. Annis (eds.) (Amsterdam: Swets & Zeitlinger).

Bhachu, Parminder K. (1986), 'Work, Dowry, and Marriage among East African Sikh Women in the United Kingdom', in *International Migration: The Female Experience*, Rita James Simon and Caroline B. Brettell (eds.) (New Jersey: Rowman & Allanheld), pp. 229–40.

Bhardwaj, Surinder M. (1990), 'Transference and Development of Sacred Space: The South Indian Example in North America', at the South Asia Conference at the University of Wisconsin, Madison.

Bhardwaj, Surinder M. and N. Madhusudana Rao (1990), 'Asian Indians in the United States: A Geographic Appraisal', in *South Asians Overseas: Migration and Ethnicity*, Colin Clarke, Ceri Peach and Steven Vertovec (eds.) (Cambridge: Cambridge University Press).

Bhardwaj, Surinder M. and G. Rinschede (1988), *Pilgrimage in World Religions* (Berlin: D. Reimer).

Bhattacharjee, Anannya (1992), 'The Habit of Ex-nomination: Nation, Woman, and the Indian Immigrant Bourgeoisie', in *Public Culture*, 5, 1 (Fall), pp. 19–44.

Bilhartz, Terry (1991), 'Sex and the Second Great Awakening: The Feminization of American Religion', in *Belief and Behavior: Essays in the New Religious History*, Philip R. Vandermeer and Robert P. Swierenga (eds.) (New Brunswick: Rutgers University Press).

Brown, Karen McCarthy (1985), 'On Feminist Methodology', *Journal of Feminist Studies in Religion*, 1, pp. 76–9.

Browner, C.H. and Dixie L. King (1989), 'Cross-cultural Perspectives on Women and Migration', *Women's Studies*, 17, pp. 49–51.

Burghart, Richard (ed.) (1987), *Hinduism in Great Britain: The Perpetuation of Religion in an Alien Cultural Milieu* (London: Tavistock).

Cainkar, Louise (1988), *Palestinian Women in the United States Coping with Tradition, Change, and Alienation*, 49/11–A, Dissertation Abstracts International.

Caplan, Patricia (1985), *Class and Gender in India* (London: Tavistock Publications).

Chai, Alice Yun (1987), 'Adaptive Strategies of Recent Korean Immigrant Women in Hawaii', in *Beyond the Public/Domestic Dichotomy: Contemporary Perspectives in Women's Public Lives*, Janet Sharistanian (ed.) (New York: Greenwood Press), pp. 65–99.

Clarke, Ceri Peach and Steven Vertovec (eds.) (1990), *South Asians Overseas: Migration and Ethnicity* (Cambridge: Cambridge University Press).

Clifford, James (1988), *The Predicament of Culture: Twentieth Century Ethnography, Literature and Art* (Cambridge: Harvard University Press).

Clifford, James and George E. Marcus (eds.) (1986), *Writing Culture: The Poetics and Politics of Ethnography* (Berkeley and Los Angeles: University of California Press).

Clothey, Fred W. (1983), *Rhythm and Intent: Ritual Studies from South India* (Madras: Blackie & Son).

Cromwell, Ronald E. and Rene A. Ruiz (1978), 'The Myth of Macho Dominance in Decision-making within Mexican and Chicano Families', *Hispanic Journal of Behavior Sciences*, 1, pp. 335–73.

Dasgupta, Sathi S. (1989), *On the Trail of an Uncertain Dream: Indian Immigrant Experience in America* (New York: AMS Press).

Dasgupta, S.D. and R.S. Hegde (1988), 'The Eternal Receptacle: A Study of Mistreatment of Women in Hindi Films', in *Women in Indian Society*, Rehana Ghadially (ed.) (New Delhi: Sage).

Dasgupta, Shamita Das (1986), 'Marching to a Different Drummer? Sex Roles of Asian Indian Women in the United States', *Women and Therapy*, 5, pp. 297–311.

Dasgupta, Tania (1986), 'Looking Under the Mosaic: South Asian Immigrant Women', *Polyphony: Women and Ethnicity*, 8, 1–2, pp. 67–9.

Davidman, Lynn (1991), *Tradition in a Rootless World: Women Turn to Orthodox Judaism* (Berkeley and Los Angeles: University of California Press).

Davis, Kingsley (1988), 'Wives and Work: A Theory of the Sex-role Revolution and Its Consequences', in *Feminism, Children and the New Families*, Sanford M. Dornbusch and Myra Stroeber (eds.) (New York: Guilford Press).

Deutsch, Sarah (1987), 'Women and Intercultural Relations: The Case of Hispanic New Mexico and Colorado', *Signs: Journal of Women in Culture and Society*, 12, 4, pp. 719–39.

Dhruvarajan, Vanaja (1989), *Hindu Women and the Power of Ideology* (Massachusetts: Bergin and Garvey).

—— (1993), 'Ethnic Cultural Retention and Transmission Among First Generation Hindu Asian Indians in a Canadian Prairie City', *Journal of Comparative Family Studies*, XXIV, 1 (Spring), pp. 63–80.

Dilrio, Judith (1982), 'Feminist Fieldwork in a Masculinist Setting: Personal Problems and Methodological Issues', Paper presented at the North Central Sociological Association Meetings.

Di Stefano, Christine (1990), 'Dilemmas of Difference: Feminism, Modernity, and Postmodernism', in *Feminism/Postmodernism*, Linda J. Nicholson (ed.) (New York and London: Routledge).

Doleve-Gandelman, Tsili (1990), 'Ethiopia as a Lost, Imaginary Space: The Role of Ethiopian Jewish Women in Producing the Ethnic Identity of their Immigrant Group in Israel', in *The Other Perspective in Gender and Culture: Rewriting Women and the Symbolic*, Juliet F. MacCannell (ed.) (New York: Columbia University Press).

Douglas, Ann (1977), *The Feminization of American Culture* (New York: Knopf).

Dumon, W.A. (1981), 'The Situation of Migrant Women Workers', *International Migrations*, 19, pp. 190–209.

Durkheim, Emile (1915), *The Elementary Forms of Religious Life*, J.W. Swain (trans.) (New York: Free Press).

Falk, Nancy Auer and Rita Gross (eds.) (1989), *Unspoken Worlds* (Belmont, CA: Wadsworth Publishing).

Fenton, John Y. (1988), *Transplanting Religious Traditions: Asian Indians in America* (New York: Praeger).

Firth, R. (1973), *Symbols: Public and Private* (Ithaca: Cornell University Press).

Fish, Virginia Kemp (1986), 'The Hull House Circle: Women's Friendships and Achievements', in *Gender, Ideology, and Action*, Sharistanian (ed.), pp. 185–227.

Fisher, Maxine P. (1980), *The Indians of New York City: A Study of Immigrants from India and Pakistan* (Colombia, MO: South Asia Books).

Flax, Jane (1986), 'Gender as a Social Problem: In and For Feminist Theory', in *American Studies*, 31, pp. 193–213.

Foner, N. (1978), *Jamaica Farewell: Jamaican Migrants in London* (Berkeley: University of California Press).

Fong, S.L.M. and H. Peskin (1973), 'Sex Role Strain and Personality Adjustment of China-born Students in America: A Pilot Study', in *Asian-Americans: Psychological Perspectives*, S. Sue and N. Wagner (eds.) (Ben Lommand, CA: Science and Behavior Books).

Fraser, Nancy and Linda Nicholson (1990), 'Social Criticism without Philosophy: An Encounter between Feminism and Postmodernism', in *Feminism/Postmodernism*, Linda J. Nicholson (ed.) (New York, London: Routledge).

Gabaccia, Donna (1991), 'Immigrant Women: Nowhere at Home?', *Journal of American Ethnic History* (Summer), pp. 61–88.

Gall, Susan B. and Timothy L. Gall (1993), *Statistical Record of Asian Americans* (Detroit: Gale Research Inc).

Ganguly, Keya (1992), 'Migrant Identities: Personal Memory and the Construction of Selfhood', *Cultural Studies*, vol. 6, 1 January, pp. 27–50.

Geertz, Clifford (1973), *The Interpretation of Cultures* (New York: Basic Books).

—— (1986), 'The Uses of Diversity', *Michigan Quarterly Review*, XXV, 1 (Winter), pp. 105–23.

Gergen, Kenneth J. (1991), *The Saturated Self: Dilemmas of Identity in Contemporary Life* (New York: Basic Books).

Ghosh, Ratna (1981a), 'Social and Economic Integration of South Asian Women in Montreal, Canada', in *Women in the Family and the Economy*, G. Kurian and R. Ghosh (eds.) (Westport, Conn.: Greenwood Press), pp. 59–71.

—— (1981b), 'Minority within a Minority: Being South Asian and Female in Canada', in *Women in the Family and the Economy*, G. Kurian and R. Ghosh (eds.) (Westport, Conn.: Greenwood Press), pp. 413–26.

—— (1983), 'Sarees and the Maple Leaf: Indian Women in Canada', in *Overseas Indians: A Study in Adaptation*, George Kurian and Ratna Ghosh (eds.) (Delhi: Vikas Publishing House).

Gifford, Carolyn De Swarte (1986), 'Home Protection: The WCTU's Conversion to Woman Suffrage', in *Gender, Ideology, and Action*, Sharistanian (ed.), pp. 95–120.

Gillis, John R. (1994), *Commemorations: The Politics of National Identity* (New Jersey: Princeton University Press).

Ginsburg, Faye and Anna Lowenhaupt Tsing (eds.) (1990), *Uncertain Terms: Negotiating Gender in American Culture* (Boston: Beacon Press).

Ginwala, K.N. (1994), 'Indian Settlement, Displacement and Re-settlement in South Africa', at International Conference on the Indian Diaspora (Hyderabad: University of Hyderabad).

Glaser, Barney G. and Anselm L. Strauss (1967), *The Discovery of Grounded Theory* (Chicago: Aldine Publishing Co).

Gupta, Akhil and James Ferguson (1992), 'Beyond "Culture": Space, Identity and the Politics of Difference', *Cultural Anthropology*, 7, 1, pp. 6–23.

Haddad, Yvonne Yazbeck and Ellison Banks Findly (eds.) (1985), *Women, Religion and Social Change* (Albany: State University of New York Press).

Haddad, Y.Y. and A.T. Lumis (1987), *Islamic Values in the United States: A Comparative Study* (New York: Oxford University Press).

Hammond, Philip (1988), 'Religion and the Persistence of Identity', *Journal for the Scientific Study of Religion*, 27, pp 1–11.

Hanchett, Suzanne (1988), *Coloured Rice: Symbolic Structure in Hindu Family Festivals* (Delhi: Hindustan Publishing Corporation).

Handler, Richard (1994), 'Is "Identity" a Useful Cross-cultural Concept?', in *Commemorations: The Politics of National Identity*, John R. Gillis (ed.) (New Jersey: Princeton University Press).

Harding, Sandra (1987), 'Is There a Feminist Method?', in *Feminism and Methodology: Social Science Issues*, Sandra Harding (ed.) (Bloomington: Indiana University Press).

—— (1990), 'Feminism, Science, and the Anti-enlightenment Critiques', in *Feminism/Postmodernism*, Linda J. Nicholson (ed.) (New York and London: Routledge).

Hargrove, Barbara (1985), 'Gender, the Family, and the Sacred', in *The Sacred in a Secular Age*, Phillip E. Hammond (ed.) (Berkeley, CA: University of California Press).

Hartsock, Nancy (1983), *Money, Sex and Power: Toward a Feminist Historical Materialism* (New York and London: Longman).

—— (1987), 'Rethinking Modernism: Minority vs. Majority Issues', *Cultural Critique*, 7, pp. 187–206.

Hegde, R.S. and S.D. Dasgupta (1984), 'Convergence and Divergence from "Devi": The Model of Ideal Woman on the Indian Screen', Paper presented at the Annual Meeting of the Western Speech and Communication Association, Seattle.

Helly, Dorothy O. and Susan M. Reverby (eds.) (1987), *Gendered Domains: Rethinking Public and Private in Women's History* (Ithaca, N.Y: Cornell University Press).

Helweg, Arthur W. and Usha M. Helweg (1990), *An Immigrant Success Story: East Indians in America* (Philadelphia: University of Pennsylvania Press).

Herberg, Will (1955), *Protestant-Catholic-Jew* (Garden City, NY: Doubleday).

Hirschman, Charles (1983), 'America's Melting Pot Reconsidered', *Annual Review of Sociology*, 9, pp. 397–423.

Hochschild, Arlie R. (1983), *The Managed Heart: Commercialization of Human Feeling* (Berkeley: University of California Press).

Hochschild, Arlie with Anne Machung (1989), *The Second Shift* (New York: Avon Books).

Immigration and Naturalization Service (1982), *Statistical Yearbook of the Immigration and Naturalization Service*, United States Immigration and Naturalization Service.

Inden, Ronald B. (1990), *Imagining India* (Oxford, UK; Cambridge, MA: Basil Blackwell).

Jacobson, Doranne (1989), 'Hindu Women's Family and Household Rites in a North Indian Village', in *Unspoken Worlds*, Nancy Auer Falk and Rita Gross (eds.) (Belmont, CA: Wadsworth).

Jacobson, Helga E. (1979), 'Immigrant Women and the Community: A Perspective for Research', *Resources for Feminist Research*, 8, 3, pp. 17–21.

Jain, P.C. (1994), 'Gulf Migration and its Impact on India', at the International Conference on the Indian Diaspora (Hyderabad: University of Hyderabad).

Jain, R.K. (1993), *Indian Communities Abroad: Themes and Literature* (Delhi: Manohar).

Jameson, Fredric (1989), 'Nostalgia for the Present', *South Atlantic Quarterly*, 88, 2 (Spring), pp. 517–37.

Jenks, Chris (ed.) (1993), *Cultural Reproduction* (London and New York: Routledge).

Jenson, Jane (1988), *Passage From India: Asian Indian Immigrants in North America* (New Haven: Yale University Press).

Kakar, Sudhir (1988), 'Feminine Identity in India', in *Women in Indian Society*, Rehana Ghadially (ed.) (New Delhi: Sage).

Keohane, Nannerl O. (1987), 'Preface' to *Gendered Domains*, Helly and Reverby (eds.), pp. ix–xii.

Khan, Nasima H. (1996), 'A Global Force to Contend With', *The Economic Times*, 31 March, 15.

Kivisto, Peter A. (1992), 'Religion and the New Immigrants', in *A Future for Religion? Trends in Social Analysis*, William H. Swatos, Jr. (eds.) (Newbury Park, CA: Sage), pp. 92–107.

Klein, Renate Duelli (1983), 'How to do what we want to do: Thoughts about Feminist Methodology' in *Theories of Women's Studies*, Gloria Bowles and Renate Duelli Klein (eds.) (London, Boston: Routledge and Kegan Paul).

Knott, Kim (1987), 'Hindu Temple Rituals in Britain: The Reinterpretation of Tradition', in *Hinduism in Great Britain: The Perpetuation of Religion in an Alien Cultural Milieu*, Richard Burghart (ed.) (London: Tavistock Publications).

Kolff, Dirk H.A. (1995), 'Indian Expansion and the Indian Diaspora: The Original Context of Emigration', International Conference of the Indian Diaspora at Trinidad.

Kondapi, C. (1951), *Indians Overseas, 1838–1949* (Madras: Oxford University Press).

Krause, Azen Corinne (1978), 'Urbanization without Breakdown: Italian, Jewish and Slavic Immigrant Women in Pittsburgh, 1900–45', *Journal of Urban History*, 4, 3 (May), pp. 391–406.

Kraut, Alan M. (1979), 'Ethnic Foodways: The Significance of Food in the Designation of Cultural Boundaries between Immigrant Groups', *Journal of American Culture*, 2, 3 (Fall), pp. 409–20.

Krauter, J.F. and M. Davis (1978), *Minority Canadians: Ethnic Groups* (Toronto: Methuen).

Krieger, Susan (1985), 'Beyond "Subjectivity": The Use of Self in Social Science', in *Innovative Sources and Uses of Qualitative Data*, Meredith Goruld (ed.), Special Issue of *Qualitative Sociology*, 8, pp. 309–24.

Lagerquist, L. DeAne (1991), *In America the Men Milk the Cows: Factors of Gender, Ethnicity, and Religion in the Americanization of the Norwegian-American Women* (Brooklyn, NY: Carlson Publishing Inc).

Lavender, Abraham (1986), *Ethnic Women and Feminist Values: Toward a 'New' Value System* (New York: University Press of America).

Leonardo, Micaela di (1984), *The Varieties of Ethnic Experience: Kinship, Class and Gender among California Italian-Americans* (Ithaca: Cornell University Press).

—— (1987), 'The Female World of Cards and Holidays: Women, Families, and the Work of Kinship', in *Signs: Journal of Women in Culture and Society*, 12(3), pp. 440–53.

Lerner, Gerda (1979), *The Majority Finds Its Past: Placing Women in History* (New York: Oxford University Press).

Leslie, Julia (1991), *Roles and Rituals for Hindu Women* (Rutherford: Fairleigh Dickinson University Press).

Levin, Hannah (1980), 'Womanizing Work', *Professional Psychology*, 11, pp. 360–8.

Liddle, Joanna and Rama Joshi (1986), *Daughters of Independence: Gender, Caste and Class in India* (London: Zed Books).

Macchiwalla, Tasqeen (1990), *A Sense of Belonging: Identity and Ritual at the Muslim Community Center of Greater Pittsburgh* (Pittsburgh: University of Pittsburgh Masters' Thesis).

Malkki, Liisa (1992), 'National Geographic: The Rooting of Peoples and the Territorialization of National Identity Among Scholars and Refugees', *Cultural Anthropology*, 7, 1 (February).

Mallea, J. (1988), 'Canadian Dualism and Pluralism: Tensions, Contradictions and Emerging Resolutions', in *Ethnic Psychology: Research and Practice with Immigrants, Refugees, Native Peoples, Ethnic Groups and Sojourners*, J.W. Berry and R.C. Annis (eds.) (Amsterdam: Swets and Zeitlinger).

Mangru, Basdeo (1987), 'The Sex Disparity Ratio and its Consequences under Indenture in British Guiana', in *India in the Caribbean*, David Dabydeen and Brinsley Samaroo (eds.) (Hansib/University of Warwick: Centre for Caribbean Studies Publication).

Markus, Maria (1987), 'Women, Success and Civil Society: Submission to, or Subversion of, the Achievement Principle', in *Feminism as Critique: On the Politics of Gender*, Seyla Benhabib and Drucilla Cornell (eds.) (Minneapolis: University of Minnesota Press).

McLellan, Janet (1987), 'Religion and Ethnicity: The Role of Buddhism in Maintaining Ethnic Identity Among Tibetans in Lindsay, Ontario', *Canadian Ethnic Studies*, XIX, 1, pp. 63–76.

Mearns, David James (1995), *Shiva's Other Children: Religion and Social Identity Amongst Overseas Indians* (New Delhi: Sage).

Mehta, Rama (1970), *The Western Educated Hindu Woman* (New York: Asia Publishing House).

Menon, Parvathi (1993), 'The Woman's Question', *India Alert Bulletin*, 6, 3, pp. 16–17.

Mies, Maria (1983), 'Towards a Methodology for Feminist Research', in *Theories of Women's Studies*, Gloria Bowles and Renate Duelli Klein (eds.) (Boston: Routledge and Kegan Paul).

Miller, Randall M. and Thomas D. Marzik (1977), *Immigrants and Religion in Urban America* (Philadelphia: Temple University Press).

Minces, Juliette (1980), *The House of Obedience: Women in Arab Society* (London: Zed Books).

Mohanty, Chandra (1988), 'Under Western Eyes: Feminist Scholarship and Colonial Discourses', *Feminist Review*, 30 (Autumn).

—— (1991), 'Cartographies of Struggle: Third World Women and the Politics of Feminism', in *Third World Women and the Politics of Feminism*, Chandra Talpade Mohanty, Ann Russo and Lordes Torres (eds.) (Bloomington and Indianapolis: Indiana University Press).

Morgan, Robin (ed.) (1984), *Sisterhood is Global: The International Women's Movement Anthology* (New York: Doubleday).

Morokvasic, Mirjana (1984), 'Birds of Passage are also Women', *International Migration Review*, 18, 4 (Winter).

Nadarajah, M. (1994), 'Diaspora and Nostalgia: Towards a Semiotic Theory of the Indian Diaspora', at the International Conference on the Indian Diaspora (Hyderabad: University of Hyderabad).

Naidoo, Josephine C. (1980), 'Women of South Asian and Anglo-Saxon Origins in the Canadian Context: Self-perceptions, Socialization, Achievement, Aspirations', in *Sex Roles: Origins, Influences and Implications for Women*, Cannie Stark-Adamec (ed.) (Montreal: Eden Press), pp. 50–69.

—— (1985a), 'Contemporary South Asian Women in the Canadian Mosaic', *International Journal of Women's Studies*, 8, 4, pp. 338–50.

—— (1985b), 'Cultural Perspectives on the Adjustment of South Asian Women in Canada', in *From a Different Perspective: Studies of Behavior Across Cultures*, I.R. Lacqunes and Y.H. Poortinga (eds.) (Lisse, The Netherlands: Swets and Zeitlinger), pp. 76–92.

Naidoo, Josephine C. and J. Campbell Davis (1988), 'Canadian South Asian Women in Transition: A Dualistic View of Life', *Journal of Comparative Family Studies*, 19, pp. 311–27.

Ng, Roxana (1981), 'Constituting Ethnic Phenomenon: An Account from the Perspective of Immigrant Women', *Canadian Ethnic Studies*, XIII, 1, pp. 97–108.

—— (1986), 'Immigrant Women in Canada: A Socially Constructed Category', *Resources for Feminist Research*, XV, 1, pp. 13–15.

Oakley, Ann (1985), *Taking it Like a Woman* (New York: Random House).

Paranjpe, Anand C. (1986), 'Identity Issues Among Immigrants: Reflections on the Experience of Indo-Canadians in British Columbia', in *Tradition and Transformation: Asian Indians in America*, Richard Harvey Brown and George V. Coelho (eds.), Studies in Third World Societies Publication No. 38 (Williamsburg, VA: College of William and Mary).

Parekh, Bikhu (1993), 'Some Reflections on the Indian Diaspora', Paper at the Second Global Convention of People of Indian Origin, New Delhi.

Parsons, Talcott and R. Bales (1955), *Family, Socialization and the Interaction Process* (Glencoe, IL: The Free Press).

Pateman, Carole (1983), 'Feminist Critiques of the Public/Private Dichotomy', in *Public and Private in Social Life*, S.I. Benn and G.F. Gaus (eds.) (London and Canberra: Croom Helm and New York: St Martin's Press).

Pessar, P.R. (1984), 'The Linkage between the Household and Workplace in the Experience of Dominican Immigrant Women in the United States', *International Migration Review*, 18, pp. 1188–211.

Poonacha, Veena (1993), 'Hindutva's Hidden Agenda: Why Women Fear Religious Fundamentalism', *Economic and Political Weekly* (13 March).

Poynting, Jeremy (1987), 'Women in the Caribbean, Experience and Voice', in *India in the Caribbean*, David Dabydeen and Brinsley Samaroo (eds.) (Hansib/University of Warwick: Centre for Caribbean Studies Publication).

Pye, E.M. (1979), 'On Comparing Buddhism and Christianity', *Studies*, 5, pp. 1–20.

Ralston, Helen (1988), 'Ethnicity, Class, and Gender Among South Asian Women in Metro Halifax: An Exploratory Study', *Canadian Ethnic Studies*, XX, 3, pp. 63–83.

Ramaseshan, Geeta (1992), 'Green Card Divorces', *Sanskriti*: A Bi-monthly Publication of Indian Students in Pittsburgh, 3, 2.

Ramnarine, Tyran (1987), 'Over a Hundred Years of East Indian Disturbances on the Sugar Estates of Guyana', in *India in the Caribbean*, David Dabydeen and Brinsley Samaroo (eds.) (Hansib/University of Warwick: Centre for Caribbean Studies Publication).

Rao, V.V.P. and N. Rao (1984), 'Sex Role Attitudes of College Students in India', in *Women in International Development Series*, Working Paper No. 1 & 2, Michigan State University.

Redfield, R. Ralph Linton and M.J. Herskovits (1936), 'Memorandum on the Study of Acculturation', *American Anthropologist*, 38, pp. 149–52.

Reinharz, Shulamit with Lynn Davidman (1992), *Feminist Methods in Social Research* (New York, Oxford: Oxford University Press).

Robertson, Roland (1992), *Globalization: Social Theory and Global Culture* (Newbury Park, CA: Sage).

—— (1994), 'Globalization or Glocalization?', *The Journal of International Communication*, 1, 1.

Robinson, Sandra (1985), 'Hindu Paradigms of Women: Images and Values', in *Women, Religion and Social Change*, Haddad, Yvonne Yazbeck and Ellison Banks Findly (eds.) (Albany: State University of New York Press).

Rosaldo, Michelle Z. (1974), 'A Theoretical Overview', in *Women, Culture and Society*, Rosaldo and Louise Lamphere (eds.) (Stanford: Stanford University Press), pp. 17–42.

Rosaldo, Michelle Z. (1980), 'The Use and Abuse of Anthropology: Reflections on Feminism and Cross-cultural Understanding', *Signs: Journal of Women in Culture and Society*, 5(3), pp. 389–417.

Rosaldo, Michelle Z. and Louise Lamphere (eds.) (1974), *Women, Culture and Society* (Stanford: Stanford University Press).

Rose, Hilary (1983), 'Hand, Brain and Heart: A Feminist Epistemology for the Natural Sciences', *Signs: Journal of Women in Culture and Society*, 9(1), pp. 73–90.

Rushdie, Salman (1991), *Imaginary Homelands: Essays in Criticism* (London: Granta Books).

Said, Edward W. (1979), 'Zionism from the Standpoint of its Victims', *Social Text*, 1, pp. 7–58.

Sanskriti: Special Issue on Communalism, a Bi-monthly Publication of Indian Students in Pittsburgh, 4, 2 (August), 1993.

Saptagiri Vani: A Publication of the Sri Venkateswara Temple, Pittsburgh, 1979.

Saran, Paramatma (1985), *The Asian Indian Experience in the United States* (Cambridge, MA: Schenkman Publishing Co).

Segal, Uma (1991), 'Cultural Variables in Asian Indian Families', *Families in Society: The Journal of Contemporary Human Services*, pp. 233–41.

Sekaran, Uma (1992), *Dual-Career Families* (San Francisco, CA: Josey Bass).

Seller, Maxine Schwartz (ed.) (1981), *Immigrant Women* (Philadelphia: Temple University Press).

Seller, Maxine Schwartz (1992), 'Comment', *Journal of American Ethnic History* (Summer), pp. 60–7.

Sharistanian, Janet (ed.) (1986), *Gender, Ideology, and Action: Historical Perspectives on Women's Lives* (New York: Greenwood Press).

—— (1987), *Beyond the Public/Domestic Dichotomy: Contemporary Perspectives on Women's Public Lives* (New York: Greenwood Press).

Shepherd, Verene (1987), 'Depression in the "Tin Roof Towns": Economic Problems of Urban Indians in Jamaica', in *India in the Caribbean*, Dabydeen and Brinsley Samaroo (eds.) (Hansib/University of Warwick: Centre for Caribbean Studies Publication).

Shostak, Marjorie (1983), *Nisa: The Life and Worlds of a Kung Woman* (New York: Vintage Books).

Silvera, Makeda (1981), 'Immigrant Domestic Workers: Whose Dirty Laundry?', *Fireweed*, 9 (Winter), pp. 53–9.

Simon, Rita James and Caroline B. Brettell (eds.) (1986), *International Migration: The Female Experience* (New Jersey: Rowman & Allanheld).

Singh, I.J. (ed.) (1979), *The Other India: The Overseas Indians and their Relationship with India* (New Delhi: Arnold-Heinemann).

Smith, Dorothy E. (1974), 'Women's Perspective as a Radical Critique of Sociology', *Sociological Enquiry*, 44, pp. 7–13.

—— (1987), *The Everyday World As Problematic* (Boston: Northeastern University Press).

Smith, Esteille M. (1980), 'The Portuguese Female Immigrant: The "Marginal Man"', *International Migration Review*, 14, 1, pp. 77–92.

Smith, Timothy L. (1978), 'Religion and Ethnicity in America', *American Historical Review*, 83 (December).

Speelman, Gezina M. (1988), 'Muslim Women in the Netherlands: Islam in Transition', Research Papers — Centre for the Study of Islam and Christian-Muslim Relations.

Srinivas, M.N. (1978), *The Changing Position of Indian Women* (New Delhi: Oxford University Press).

Stacey, Judith (1988), 'Can there be a Feminist Ethnography?', *Women's Studies International Forum*, 11, pp. 21–7.

Stall, Susan (1985), '"What about the Non-Feminist?": The Possibilities of Women's Movement Coalition Building in Small Town America', Paper presented at the Annual Meeting of the Society for the Study of Social Problems.

Stein, Burton (1961), 'The State, the Temple and Agricultural Development: A Study in Medieval South India', *The Economic and Political Weekly*, 4 (February), pp. 7–26.

Strauss, Anselm L. (1987), *Qualitative Analysis for Social Scientists* (Cambridge: Cambridge University Press).

Sue, D.W. (1973), 'Ethnic Identity: The Impact of Two Cultures on the Psychological Development of Asians in America', in *Asian Americans: Psychological Perspectives*, S. Sue and N. Wagner (eds.) (Ben Lomond, CA: Science and Behavior Books), pp. 140–9.

Tinker, Hugh (1977), *The Banyan Tree: Overseas Immigrants from India, Pakistan and Bangladesh* (Oxford: Oxford University Press).

Tsing, Anna Lowenhaupt (1993), *In the Realm of the Diamond Queen* (Princeton, NJ: Princeton University Press).

Underwood, June O. (1986), 'Civilizing Kansas: Women's Organizations, 1880–1921', in *Gender, Ideology, and Action*, Sharistanian (ed.), pp. 157–84.

Wadley, Susan S. (1989), 'Hindu Women's Family and Household Rites in a North Indian Village', in *Unspoken Worlds: Women's Religious Lives in Non-Western Cultures*, Nancy A. Falk and Rita M. Gross (eds.) (San Francisco: Harper & Row).

Wajcman, Judy (1983), *Women in Control: Dilemmas of a Workers' Co-operative* (New York: St Martin's Press).

Warner, Stephen R. (1988), *New Wine in Old Wineskins* (Berkeley and Los Angeles: University of California Press).

—— (1993a), 'Works in Progress Toward a New Paradigm for the Sociological Study of Religion in the United States', *American Journal of Sociology*, 98, 5 (March), pp. 1044–93.

Warner, Stephen R. (1993b), *The New Ethnic and Immigrant Congregations Project Proposal* (Chicago: University of Illinois).

Weinberg, Sydney Stahl (1988), *The World of Our Mothers: The Lives of Jewish Immigrant Women* (Chapel Hill: University of North Carolina Press).

—— (1992), 'The Treatment of Women in Immigration History: A Call for Change', *Journal of American Ethnic History* (Summer), pp. 25–46.

Weiting, Stephen G. (1975), 'An Examination of Intergenerational Patterns of Religious Belief and Practice', *Sociological Analysis*, 36, 2, pp. 137–49.

Williams, Raymond (1988), *Religions of Immigrants from India and Pakistan: New Threads in the American Tapestry* (Cambridge: Cambridge University Press).

Wilson, Amrit (1978), *Finding A Voice: Asian Women in Britain* (London: Virago).

Woolgar, Steve (1988), *Knowledge and Reflexivity: New Frontiers in the Sociology of Knowledge* (London, Newbury Park: Sage).

Wuthnow, Robert (1988), 'Sociology of Religion', in *Handbook of Sociology*, Neil J. Smelser (ed.) (Newbury Park, CA: Sage).

Young, Iris Marion (1987), 'Impartiality and the Civic Public: Some Implications of Feminist Critiques of Moral and Political Theory', in *Feminism as Critique*, Seyla Benhabib and Drucilla Cornell (eds.) (Minneapolis: University of Minnesota Press).

Zinn, Maxine Baca (1979), 'Chicano Family Research: Conceptual Distortions and Alternative Directions', *Journal of Ethnic Studies*, 7 (Fall), pp. 59–71.

Zuhur, Sherifa (1992), *Revealing Reveiling: Islamic Gender Ideology in Egypt* (Albany: Suny Press).

Index